Weekend
Quilting
Wonders™

Edited by Jeanne Stauffer & Sandra L. Hatch

HOUSE of
WHITE
BIRCHES
PUBLISHERS
SINCE 1947

Weekend Quilting Wonders™

EDITORS	Jeanne Stauffer, Sandra L. Hatch
ART DIRECTOR	Brad Snow
PUBLISHING SERVICES DIRECTOR	Brenda Gallmeyer
ASSOCIATE EDITOR	Dianne Schmidt
ASSISTANT ART DIRECTOR	Nick Pierce
COPY SUPERVISOR	Michelle Beck
COPY EDITORS	Sue Harvey, Nicki Lehman, Judy Weatherford
TECHNICAL ARTIST	Connie Rand
GRAPHIC ARTS SUPERVISOR	Ronda Bechinski
GRAPHIC ARTIST	Nicole Gage
BOOK DESIGN	Amy S. Lin
PRODUCTION ASSISTANT	Marj Morgan, Judy Neuenschwander
PHOTOGRAPHY SUPERVISOR	Tammy Christian
PHOTOGRAPHY	Don Clark, Matt Owen, Jackie Shaffel
PHOTO STYLISTS	Tammy Nussbaum, Tammy N. Smith
CHIEF EXECUTIVE OFFICER	David J. McKee
MARKETING DIRECTOR	Dwight Seward

Printed in China
First Printing: 2007
Library of Congress Control Number: 2006932191
Hardcover ISBN: 978-1-59217-164-4
Softcover ISBN: 978-1-59217-165-1

1 2 3 4 5 6 7 8 9

Introduction

Can you think of a better way to spend a weekend than to spend it quilting, making a project for your home or a gift for someone you love?

When selecting the designs for this book, we chose a wide range of projects, from table runners that you can make from start to finish in a few hours to a full-size quilt that may take two or three weekends, depending on your skill level. Of course, if you are an experienced quilter, you can probably make all but one quilt in this collection in only one weekend if you've already purchased the fabric and supplies and read through the instructions. Start on Friday evening, and you'll be done before the weekend is over.

You'll love making the soft and dreamy baby quilts and the bright knock-your-socks-off quilts for toddlers. Dragonflies and Scotty dogs are favorites for these quilts. A Doggie Dreams dog bed cover is also included.

Throws to cover Grandma's knees and to cuddle up in are included for everyone. Bed-size quilts that can be completed in one weekend are also included. There are lots of choices for teens and adults.

It's never too soon to begin making Christmas quilts and Christmas decorations. A Rudolph gift bag, Christmas Rose Skinny Scarf and 84" x 99" Christmas Ribbons bed quilt start off the selection of holiday projects. Make these projects to decorate your own home and a second version to give as a gift.

For those of you who would rather spend your evenings quilting, we've included many table decorations. Tree Time table topper and coasters will help you celebrate the holidays. A 32"-square Tulip Carousel topper and a 45"-square Pansy topper usher in the beauty of spring. There are quilted table runners and toppers for every occasion.

We haven't told you about half of the over 40 projects in this book, but it's time to start planning for the weekend. So pick out the first project you want to make and have a wonderful time quilting. We wish you many fun quilting weekends in the months ahead.

Happy quilting,

Jeanne Stauffer
Sandra L. Hatch

Contents

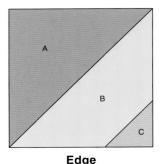

Edge
6" x 6" Block
Make 24

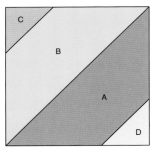

Center
6" x 6" Block
Make 24

Grandma's Joy

Two easy blocks and flannel prints stitch up in a weekend making this lap-size quilt to keep your little one warm.

DESIGN BY JULIE WEAVER

Project Specifications
Skill Level: Beginner
Quilt Size: 50" x 62"
Block Size: 6" x 6"
Number of Blocks: 48

Materials
All fabrics are flannel
- ⅓ yard blue dot
- 1 yard yellow print
- 1¼ yards yellow dot
- 1¾ yards blue print
- Backing 56" x 68"
- Batting 56" x 68"
- All-purpose thread to match fabrics
- Quilting thread
- Basic sewing tools and supplies

Cutting
Step 1. Cut four 6⅞" by fabric width strips each blue (A) and yellow (B) prints; subcut strips into (24) 6⅞" squares each fabric.

Step 2. Cut five 5½" by fabric width strips blue print.

Join strips on short ends to make one long strip; press seams open. Subcut strip into two 52½" G strips and two 40½" H strips.

Step 3. Cut three 2½" by fabric width strips blue dot; subcut strips into (48) 2½" C squares. Draw a diagonal line from corner to corner on the wrong side of each square.

Step 4. Cut two 2½" by fabric width strips yellow dot; subcut strips into (24) 2½" D squares. Draw a diagonal line from corner to corner on the wrong side of each square.

Step 5. Cut five 2½" by fabric width strips yellow dot. Join strips on short ends to make one long strip; press seams open. Subcut strip into two 48½" E strips and two 40½" F strips.

Step 6. Cut one 5½" by fabric width strip yellow dot; subcut strip into four 5½" I squares.

Step 7. Cut six 2½" by fabric width strips yellow dot for binding.

Completing the A-B Units
Step 1. Draw a diagonal line on the wrong side of each B square. Place a B square right sides together with an A

square and stitch ¼" on each side of the marked line as shown in Figure 1. Repeat for all A and B squares.

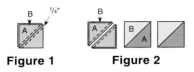

Figure 1   **Figure 2**

Step 2. Cut each stitched unit apart on the marked lines to make A-B units as shown in Figure 2; press seams toward A.

Completing the Edge Blocks

Step 1. Place a C square right sides together on the corner of B and stitch on the marked line as shown in Figure 3.

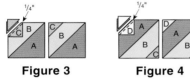

Figure 3   **Figure 4**

Step 2. Trim seam allowance to ¼" and press C to the right side to complete one Edge block, again referring to Figure 3; repeat to make 24 Edge blocks.

Completing the Center Blocks

Step 1. Repeat Steps 1 and 2 for Completing the Edge Blocks with remaining A-B units and C squares.
Step 2. Place a D square right sides together on the corner of A and stitch on the marked line as shown in Figure 4.
Step 3. Trim seam allowance to ¼" and press D to the right side to complete one Center block, again referring to Figure 4; repeat to make 24 Center blocks.

Completing the Quilt

Step 1. Arrange six Edge blocks to make an X row as shown in Figure 5; press seams in one direction. Repeat to make two X rows.

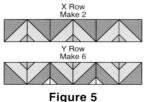

Figure 5

Step 2. Join two Edge blocks with four Center blocks to make a Y row, again referring to Figure 5; press seams in the opposite direction from the X rows. Repeat to make six Y rows.
Step 3. Join the X and Y rows referring to the Placement Diagram for positioning of rows; press seams in one direction.
Step 4. Sew an E strip to opposite long sides and F strips to the top and bottom of the pieced center; press seams toward E and F strips.
Step 5. Sew a G strip to opposite long sides of the pieced center; press seams toward G strips.
Step 6. Sew an I square to each end of each H strip; press seams toward H strips.
Step 7. Sew an H-I strip to the top and bottom of the pieced center to complete the pieced top; press seams toward the H-I strips.
Step 8. Complete the quilt referring to Completing Your Quilt on page 170. ❖

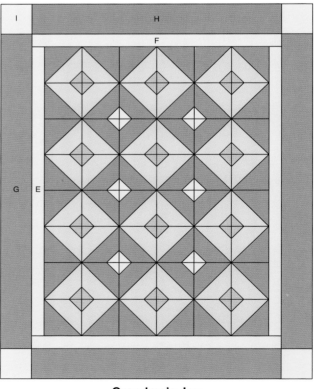

Grandma's Joy
Placement Diagram
50" x 62"

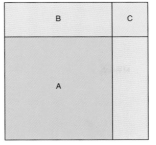

Sweet Pink
8" x 8" Block
Make 18

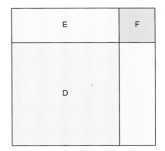

Sweet Yellow
8" x 8" Block
Make 18

Soft & Sweet

Luscious chenilles and embossed-fleece fabrics make this soft throw.

DESIGN BY JILL REBER

Project Specifications
Skill Level: Beginner
Quilt Size: 60" x 60"
Block Size: 8" x 8"
Number of Blocks: 36

Materials
- ¼ yard each yellow tonal and pink dot
- ½ yard pink embossed fleece (60" wide)
- ½ yard yellow/pink plaid
- ⅝ yard yellow chenille
- ⅝ yard each yellow and pink checks
- 1¼ yards yellow/pink floral
- Backing 66" x 66"
- Batting 66" x 66"
- All-purpose thread to match fabrics
- Quilting thread
- Pink and yellow pearl cotton
- Basic sewing tools and supplies

Cutting
Step 1. Cut (18) 6½" x 6½" squares each pink embossed fleece (A) and yellow chenille (D).
Step 2. Cut three 6½" by fabric width strips each pink (B) and yellow (E) checks; subcut strips into 36 each 2½" B and E rectangles.

Step 3. Cut two 2½" by fabric width strips each pink dot (C) and yellow tonal (F); subcut strips into 18 each 2½" C and F squares.

Step 4. Cut six 6½" by fabric width strips yellow/pink floral. Join strips on the short ends to make one long strip; press seams open. Subcut strips into two 48½" G strips and two 60½" H strips.

Step 5. Cut six 2¼" by fabric width strips yellow/pink plaid for binding.

Completing the Blocks

Step 1. To complete one Sweet Pink block, sew B to one side of A; press seam toward B.

Step 2. Sew C to one end of B; press seam toward B.

Step 3. Sew the B-C unit to the A-B unit as shown in Figure 1 to complete one block; press seam toward B-C. Repeat to make 18 blocks.

Figure 1   **Figure 2**

Step 4. Repeat Steps 1–3 with D, E and F pieces referring to Figure 2 to complete 18 Sweet Yellow blocks, pressing seams toward E.

Completing the Quilt

Step 1. Join three each Sweet Yellow and Sweet Pink blocks as shown in Figure 3 to make a row; press seams toward Sweet Pink blocks. Repeat to make six rows.

Figure 3

Step 2. Join the rows referring to the Placement Diagram for positioning; press seams in one direction.

Step 3. Sew G strips to opposite sides and H strips to the remaining sides of the pieced center to complete the top; press seams toward the G and H strips.

Step 4. Quilt and bind the quilt referring to Completing Your Quilt on page 170. Using 3 strands of pink pearl cotton, tie a knot in the center of each pink A square; trim ends to ½". Repeat with yellow pearl cotton in the yellow D squares. ❖

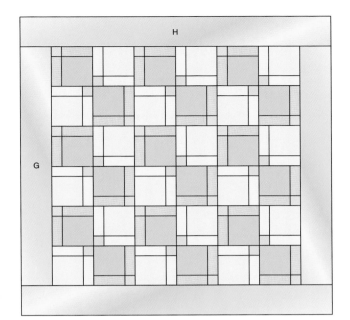

Soft & Sweet
Placement Diagram
60" x 60"

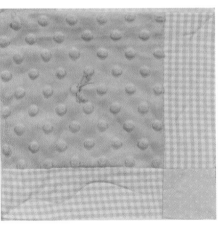

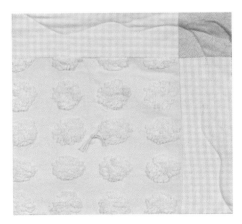

Little Miss Toy Tote

Add 3-D shapes to turn a simple bag into an elegant toy tote.

DESIGN BY CONNIE KAUFFMAN

Project Specifications
Skill Level: Beginner
Tote Size: 7¼" x 7½" x 3"

Materials
- Scraps yellow and pink
- ⅛ yard each blue and lime green tonals
- ⅛ yard butterfly print
- ½ yard pink dot tonal
- Batting 12" x 19"
- All-purpose thread to match fabrics
- Quilting thread
- Gold metallic and colored decorative threads
- 8½" x 11" sheet double-sided fusible web
- 1 (⅝") hook-and-loop circle
- 4 (1") white flower buttons
- Basic sewing tools and supplies

Cutting
Step 1. Cut one 11½" x 11" A piece and one 12" x 19" backing piece pink dot tonal.

Step 2. Cut two 1⅛" x 11" binding strips pink dot tonal.

Step 3. Cut two 1" x 11" B strips and one 1¼" x 6" strip blue tonal.

Step 4. Cut two 1" x 11" C strips and two 12" x 3" handle strips lime green tonal.

Step 5. Cut two 3" x 11" D strips butterfly print.

Step 6. Trace one each flower and butterfly shape onto one paper side of the fusible web; cut out shapes, leaving a ½" margin around each one. Remove paper from one side of the cut shapes.

Step 7. Using an iron, place the shapes fusible side down on the wrong side of the fabric as directed on patterns for color; fuse in place.

Step 8. Remove the top paper and fold the excess fabric wrong sides together over the fused area and press.

Step 9. Place the fusible paper with the traced design over the fused fabric and cut out the design. ***Note:*** *You will now have a double-sided fabric shape.*

Completing the Tote

Step 1. Join the A, B, C and D strips to complete the pieced top as shown in Figure 1; press seams toward A.

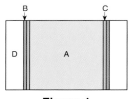
Figure 1

Step 2. Sandwich the batting between the pieced top and the 12" x 19" backing piece; pin to hold.

Step 3. Quilt as desired by hand or machine.

Step 4. Trim batting and backing even with the pieced top.

Step 5. Press under ¼" on one long edge of each binding strip; sew a binding strip to each raw short end. Turn binding strips to the backing side over seam and hand-stitch in place.

Step 6. Fold the quilted top with wrong sides together and sew ⅛" along each long side as shown in Figure 2.

Figure 2

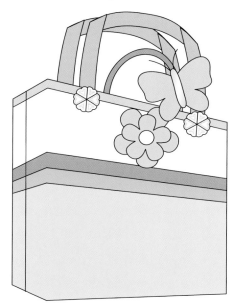
Little Miss Toy Tote
Placement Diagram
7¼" x 7½" x 3"

Step 7. Turn the bag backing side out; stitch a ¼" seam along the previously stitched edges to enclose the seam as shown in Figure 3.

Figure 3

Step 8. Fold one bottom corner of the bag to form a point with the side seam centered as shown in Figure 4.

Figure 4

Step 9. Sew 1½" from the point as shown in Figure 5; repeat on the remaining side seam to make a square bottom on the bag. Turn right side out.

Figure 5

Step 10. Fold each 12" x 3" handle strip with long edges toward the center of the strip and press referring to Figure 6; fold strip in half and press, again referring to Figure 6.

Figure 6

Step 11. Sew close to the folded edges of each handle strip; zigzag across the raw ends.

Step 12. Hand-tack the handle strips to the top inside edge of the bag about 2" from the side seams as shown in Figure 7.

Figure 7

Step 13. Repeat Steps 10 and 11 with the 1¼" x 6" strip blue tonal to make the closing strap.

Step 14. Hand-stitch the closing strap to the inside top center of one side of the bag as shown in Figure 8.

Figure 8

Step 15. Using the gold metallic and other decorative threads, sew along the butterfly's body to add some color and dimension. Leave ends of the gold metallic thread 5" long; tie a knot in the end and trim to make butterfly antennae about 1¼" long.

Step 16. Sew the butterfly to the unstitched end of the blue strap. Hand-stitch the hook part of the hook-and-loop circle to the wrong side of the butterfly shape.

Step 17. Place the large flower on the outside of the tote, matching the flower center with the area where the hook circle on the butterfly will lie; lay the smaller flower on top of the larger one. Hand-stitch in place through the center of the flowers to secure.

Step 18. Hand-stitch the loop circle to the center of the flowers.

Step 19. Sew a 1" white flower button over the area where the handles are attached to the bag to finish referring to the Placement Diagram for positioning. ❖

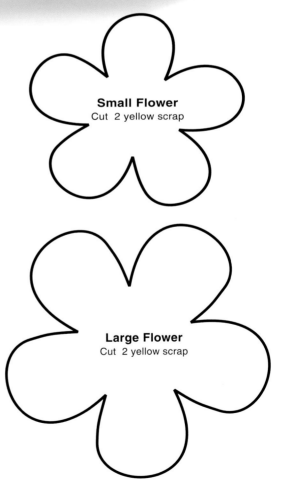

Small Flower
Cut 2 yellow scrap

Butterfly
Cut 2 pink scrap

Large Flower
Cut 2 yellow scrap

Lullaby
9" x 12" Block

Lullaby

Sew up a welcome quilt for a baby in a snap with fast-and-easy strip piecing.

DESIGN BY JULIE WEAVER

Project Specifications

Skill Level: Beginner
Quilt Size: 44" x 53"
Block Size: 9" x 12"
Number of Blocks: 9

Materials

All fabrics are flannel
- ⅝ yard cream star print
- 1 yard pink print
- 1 yard pink dot
- 1⅓ yards green print
- Backing 50" x 59"
- Batting 50" x 59"
- All-purpose thread to match fabrics
- Quilting thread
- Basic sewing tools and supplies

Cutting

Step 1. Cut two 3½" by fabric width A strips and four 2½" by fabric width I strips pink print.
Step 2. Cut two 1½" x 40½" M strips and two 1½" x 33½" N strips pink print.
Step 3. Cut five 1½" by fabric width strips pink print. Join strips on short ends to make one long strip; press

seams open. Subcut strip into two 51½" R strips and two 44½" S strips.
Step 4. Cut eight 1½" by fabric width strips green print for B and H.
Step 5. Cut two 2½" by fabric width F strips and one 3½" by fabric width D strip green print.
Step 6. Cut one 1½" by fabric width strip green print; subcut strip into (16) 1½" K squares.
Step 7. Cut two 5" x 33½" P strips and two 5" x 42½" O strips green print.
Step 8. Cut four 2½" by fabric width C strips and two 3½" by fabric width G strips cream star print.
Step 9. Cut two 1½" by fabric width E strips pink dot.
Step 10. Cut seven 1½" by fabric width strips pink dot; subcut strips into 12 each 9½" J and 12½" L strips.
Step 11. Cut one 5" by fabric width strip pink dot; subcut strip into four 5" Q squares.
Step 12. Cut five 2½" by fabric width strips pink dot for binding.

Completing the Blocks

Step 1. Sew a B and then C strip to opposite sides of A with right sides together along the length to make an A-B-C strip set; press seams away from A. Repeat to make two A-B-C strip sets.

Step 2. Subcut the A-B-C strip sets into nine 6½" A-B-C units as shown in Figure 1.

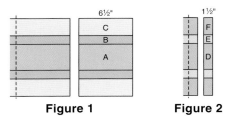

Figure 1   **Figure 2**

Step 3. Repeat Step 1 with E and F strips on each side of D to make one D-E-F strip set; press seams toward E.
Step 4. Subcut the D-E-F strip set into (18) 1½" D-E-F units as shown in Figure 2.
Step 5. Repeat Step 1 with H and I strips on each side of G to make two G-H-I strip sets; press seams away from G.
Step 6. Subcut the G-H-I strip sets into (18) 2½" G-H-I units as shown in Figure 3.

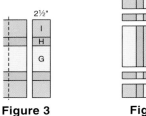

Figure 3   **Figure 4**

Step 7. To complete one Lullaby block, sew a D-E-F unit to opposite short sides of an A-B-C unit as shown in Figure 4; press seams away from the A-B-C unit.
Step 8. Sew a G-H-I unit to opposite short sides of the pieced unit to complete one block, again referring to Figure 4; press seams toward the G-H-I units. Repeat to make nine blocks.

Completing the Quilt
Step 1. Join three blocks with four L strips to make a block row referring to Figure 5; press seams toward the L strips. Repeat to make three block rows.

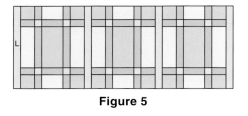

Figure 5

Step 2. Join three J strips and four K squares to make a sashing row as shown in Figure 6; press seams toward the J strips. Repeat to make four sashing rows.

Figure 6

Step 3. Join the block rows with the sashing rows, beginning and ending with a sashing row to complete the pieced center; press seams toward the sashing rows.
Step 4. Sew an M strip to opposite long sides and N strips to the top and bottom of the pieced center; press seams toward the M and N strips.
Step 5. Sew an O strip to opposite long sides of the pieced center; press seams toward the O strips.
Step 6. Sew Q to each end of each P strip; press seams toward the P strips.
Step 7. Sew a P-Q strip to the top and bottom of the pieced center; press seams toward the P-Q strips.
Step 8. Sew an R strip to opposite long sides and S strips to the top and bottom of the pieced center; press seams toward the R and S strips to complete the top.
Step 9. Complete the quilt referring to Completing Your Quilt on page 170. ❖

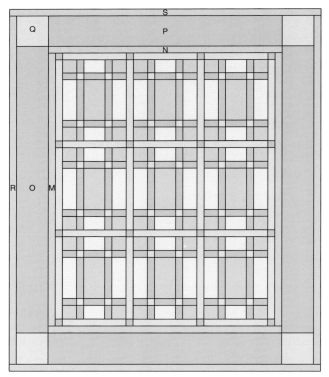

Lullaby
Placement Diagram
44" x 53"

Dragonfly Baby Quilt

Use a fusible grid to create a quick-to-stitch baby quilt.

DESIGN BY JUDITH SANDSTROM

Project Specifications
Skill Level: Beginner
Quilt Size: 43" x 48"

Materials
- ¼ yard each gold multicolor dot and gold tonal
- ¼ yard white tonal
- ⅓ yard each gold and green tonals
- ⅜ yard purple tonal
- ½ yard gold print
- ½ yard blue tonal
- ¾ yard orange tonal
- Backing 49" x 54"
- Batting 49" x 54"
- All-purpose thread to match fabrics
- Quilting thread
- ¼ yard fusible web
- ¼ yard fabric stabilizer
- 1⅜ yards fusible web with a 1" grid
- Basic sewing tools and supplies

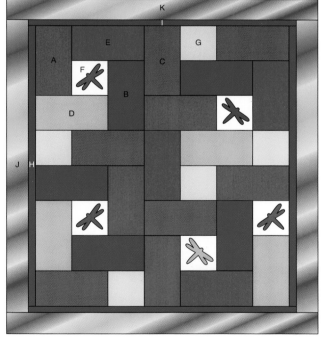

Dragonfly Baby Quilt
Placement Diagram
43" x 48"

Cutting
Step 1. Trace five dragonfly appliqué shapes onto the paper side of the fusible web. Cut out shapes, leaving a margin around each one.

Step 2. Fuse shapes to the wrong side of fabrics as directed on the pattern for color and number to cut. Cut out shapes on traced lines; remove paper backing.

Step 3. Cut two 5" by fabric width strips each orange (A), blue (B) and purple (C) tonals; subcut strips into five 10" rectangles each fabric.

Step 4. Cut one 5" by fabric width strip each gold (D) and green (E) tonals; subcut strips into four 10" rectangles each fabric.

Step 5. Cut one 5" by fabric width strip each white tonal (F) and gold multicolor dot (G); subcut strips into five 5" squares each fabric.

Step 6. Cut two strips each 1" x 40" H and 1" x 37" I blue tonal.

Step 7. Cut five 3" by fabric width strips gold print. Join strips on short ends to make one long strip; press seams open. Subcut strips into two 42" J strips and two 43" K strips.

Step 8. Cut five 2¼" by fabric width strips orange tonal for binding.

Step 9. Cut five 5" x 5" squares fabric stabilizer.

Completing the Quilt

Step 1. Center and fuse a dragonfly shape onto each F square referring to the Placement Diagram for positioning.

Step 2. Pin a fabric stabilizer square to the wrong side of each fused square. Using thread to match the dragonfly shapes, machine zigzag-stitch around each shape; pull thread to the wrong side, knot ends and trim.

Step 3. Remove the fabric stabilizer.

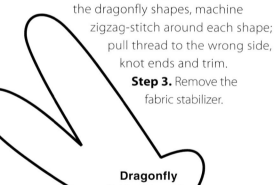

Dragonfly
Cut 1 each purple, blue, green, gold & orange tonals

Step 4. Lay the gridded fusible web out on a large, firm ironable surface with the bumpy, fusible side up.

Step 5. Referring to the Placement Diagram for positioning, place the squares and rectangles on top of the gridded fusible web so that edges meet but do not overlap. *Note: Be sure to allow 4" on each side and ends for borders. Also note that the dragonflies are facing in different directions.*

Step 6. When all squares are perfectly aligned, fuse in place referring to the gridded fusible web manufacturer's instructions. *Note: Be careful not to place the hot iron on the uncovered edges of the gridded fusible web.*

Step 7. Arrange and fuse the H strips to opposite long sides and I strips to the top and bottom of the fused center.

Step 8. Arrange and fuse the J strips to opposite long sides and K strips to the top and bottom of the fused center; trim any excess fusible gridded web even with the border edges, if necessary.

Step 9. Sandwich the batting between the fused quilt top and the prepared backing piece; baste the layers together with vertical and horizontal lines and around edges. Trim excess batting and backing even with the quilt-top edges.

Step 10. Using thread to match fabric and stitching one color at a time, machine zigzag-stitch around each square, rectangle and strip referring to photo.

Step 11. Bind the quilt referring to Completing Your Quilt on page 170. ❖

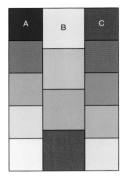

Rainbow
6½" x 10" Block

Rainbow Baby Quilt

Bright-color fabric strips make up the simple blocks in this eye-catching baby quilt. It's a great way to add color to your baby's room.

DESIGN BY CONNIE RAND

Project Specifications
Skill Level: Beginner
Quilt Size: 50½" x 55"
Block Size: 6½" x 10"
Number of Blocks: 20

Materials
- ½ yard each 5 different blue and green novelty prints from light to dark
- ½ yard each orange, gold and yellow prints or solids
- ¾ yard red print
- Backing 57" x 61"
- Batting 57" x 61"
- Neutral color all-purpose thread
- Quilting thread
- Basic sewing tools and supplies

Cutting
Step 1. Cut two 2½" by fabric width strips from each of the five blue (A) and green (C) fabrics.
Step 2. Cut two 3" by fabric width B strips each red print and orange, gold and yellow fabrics.

Step 3. Cut six 3½" x 10½" D rectangles each from gold and yellow and medium and dark blue fabrics.
Step 4. Cut five 3½" x 7" E rectangles each red, dark blue and orange and light and dark green fabrics.
Step 5. Cut six 3½" x 3½" F squares each orange, gold and dark green and medium and dark blue fabrics.
Step 6. Cut six 2¼" by fabric width strips red print for binding.

Completing the Blocks
Step 1. Join one of each A strip with right sides together along the length to make a strip set as shown in Figure 1; repeat to make two A strip sets. Press seams in one direction.
Step 2. Subcut the A strip sets into (20) 2½" A units, again referring to Figure 1.

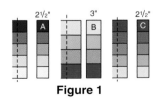

Figure 1

Step 3. Repeat Steps 1 and 2 with the C strips to make (20) 2½" C units, again referring to Figure 1.

Step 4. Repeat Step 1 with B strips; subcut strip sets into (20) 3" B units, again referring to Figure 1.

Step 5. Join one each A, B and C strips as shown in Figure 2 to complete one Rainbow block; press seams in one direction. Repeat to make 20 blocks.

Figure 2

Completing the Quilt

Step 1. Join five Rainbow blocks with six medium blue D strips to make a medium blue row referring to Figure 3; press seams toward D.

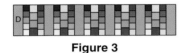

Figure 3

Rainbow Baby Quilt
Placement Diagram
50½" x 55"

Step 2. Repeat Step 1 with remaining D pieces to make one each gold, yellow and dark blue rows referring to the Placement Diagram; press seams toward D.

Step 3. Join five red E pieces with six gold F squares to make a sashing row as shown in Figure 4; press seams toward E. Repeat to make five sashing rows, again referring to Figure 4.

Step 4. Join the block rows with the sashing rows referring to the Placement Diagram for color positioning; press seams toward the sashing rows to complete the top.

Step 5. Complete the quilt referring to Completing Your Quilt on page 170. ❖

Figure 4

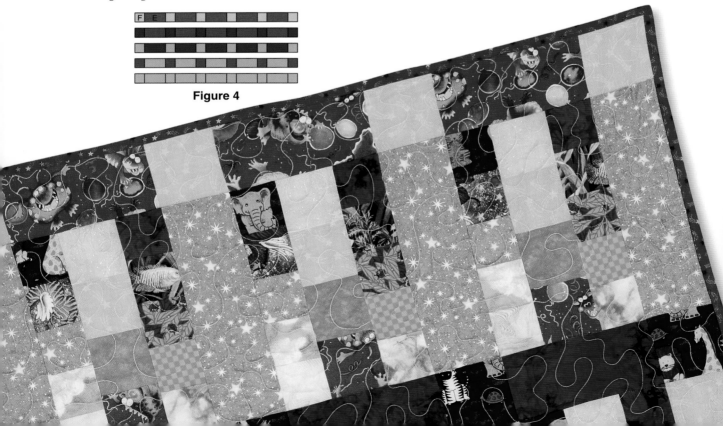

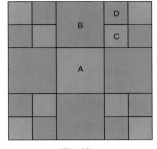

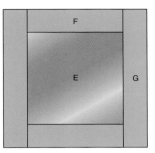

Thrifty
9" x 9" Block
Make 8

Focus
9" x 9" Block
Make 7

Neon Fabric Fun

Build a quilt around a cute novelty print using two simple pieced blocks.

DESIGN BY JILL REBER

Project Specifications

Skill Level: Beginner
Quilt Size: 39" x 57"
Block Size: 9" x 9"
Number of Blocks: 15

Materials

- ½ yard orange dot
- ⅔ yard blue dot
- ¾ yard green multidot
- 1¾ yards focus fabric
- Backing 45" x 63"
- Batting 45" x 63"
- All-purpose thread to match fabrics
- Quilting thread
- Basic sewing tools and supplies

Cutting

Note: *A directional print was used as the focus fabric for this quilt.*

Step 1. Cut one 3½" by fabric width strip orange dot; subcut strip into eight 3½" A squares.

Step 2. Cut four 2" by fabric width strips each orange (C) and blue (D) dots.

Step 3. Cut three 3½" by fabric width strips blue dot; subcut strips into (32) 3½" B squares.

Step 4. Cut two 6½" x 57½" I strips along the length of the focus fabric.

Step 5. Cut two 6½" x 27½" H strips and seven 6½" E squares across the remaining width of the focus fabric.

Step 6. Cut six 2" by fabric width strips green multidot; subcut strips into (14) 6½" F strips and (14) 9½" G strips.

Step 7. Cut five 2¼" by fabric width strips green multidot for binding.

Piecing the Thrifty Blocks

Step 1. Sew a C strip to a D strip with right sides together along the length; press seams toward D. Repeat to make four C-D strip sets.

Step 2. Subcut the C-D strip sets into (64) 2" C-D units as shown in Figure 1.

Figure 1

Step 3. Join two C-D units as shown in Figure 2 to make a corner unit; press seam in one direction. Repeat to make 32 corner units.

Figure 2

Step 4. To complete one Thrifty block, sew B to opposite sides of A to make an A-B row as shown in Figure 3; press seams toward B.

Figure 3

Step 5. Sew a corner unit to opposite sides of B to make a B-C-D row, again referring to Figure 3; press seams toward B. Repeat to make two rows.

Step 6. Sew the A-B row between the two B-C-D rows to complete one block referring to the block drawing; press seams toward the A-B row. Repeat to make eight Thrifty blocks.

Completing the Focus Blocks

Step 1. To complete one Focus block, sew F to the top and bottom of E; press seams toward F.

Step 2. Sew G to opposite sides of the E-F unit to complete one block; press seams toward F. Repeat to make seven Focus blocks.

Completing the Quilt

Step 1. Join two Thrifty blocks with one Focus block to make an X row as shown in Figure 4; press seams toward the Focus block. Repeat to make three X rows.

Neon Fabric Fun
Placement Diagram
39" x 57"

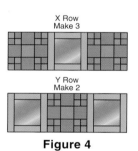

X Row
Make 3

Y Row
Make 2

Figure 4

Step 2. Join two Focus blocks with one Thrifty block to make a Y row, again referring to Figure 4; press seams toward the Focus blocks. Repeat to make two Y rows.

Step 3. Join the X and Y rows to complete the pieced center referring to the Placement Diagram for positioning of rows; press seams in one direction.

Step 4. Sew an H strip to the top and bottom and I strips to opposite long sides of the pieced center to complete the pieced top; press seams toward the H and I strips.

Step 5. Complete the quilt referring to Completing Your Quilt on page 170. ❖

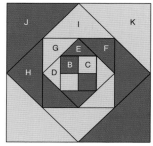

Snail's Trail
9" x 9" Block
Make 1

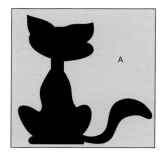

Cat
9" x 9" Block
Make 2

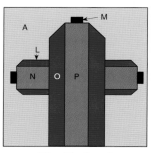

Fire Hydrant
9" x 9" Block
Make 2

Doggie Dreams

If dogs do dream, they might be dreaming about fire hydrants and the fun of chasing cats on this dog-bed pillow cover.

DESIGN BY LUCY A. FAZELY & MICHAEL L. BURNS

Project Specifications
Skill Level: Intermediate
Quilt Size: 30" x 30"
Block Size: 9" x 9"
Number of Blocks: 5

Materials
- 8" x 12" scrap medium red tonal
- 12" x 14" scrap dark red tonal
- ⅓ yard black tonal
- ⅓ yard medium green tonal
- ¾ yard light green print
- 1⅓ yards dark green tonal
- Batting 31" x 31"
- Lining 31" x 31"
- Neutral color all-purpose thread
- Clear nylon monofilament
- Quilting thread
- 30" x 30" dog-bed pillow
- 1 yard 12"-wide fusible web
- Appliqué pressing sheet
- Basting spray
- Basic sewing tools and supplies

Doggie Dreams
Placement Diagram
30" x 30"

Cutting

Step 1. Trace the cat pattern onto the paper side of the fusible web as directed on the pattern; cut out shapes, leaving a margin around each one.

Step 2. Fuse paper shapes to the wrong side of the black solid; cut out shapes on traced lines. Remove paper backing.

Step 3. Cut one 9½" by fabric width strip light green print; subcut strip into four 9½" A squares.

Step 4. Cut one 14" by fabric width strip light green print; subcut strip into one 14" square. Cut the square on both diagonals to make four R triangles.

Step 5. From the remainder of the strip cut in Step 4, cut two 1⅝" x 1⅝" C squares and one each 2½" x 2½" D, 3⅛" x 3⅛" G, 4" x 4" I and 5⅜" x 5⅜" K squares. Cut all except the C squares in half on one diagonal to make two triangles from each square.

Step 6. Cut one 7¼" by fabric width strip medium green tonal; subcut strip into two each 7¼" Q and 1⅝" x 1⅝" B squares and one each 2½" x 2½" E, 3⅛" x 3⅛" F, 4" x 4" H and 5⅜" x 5⅜" J squares. Cut all except the B squares in half on one diagonal to make two triangles from each square.

Step 7. Cut two 3" x 26" S strips and two 3" x 31" T strips dark green tonal.

Step 8. Cut one 31" by fabric width strip dark green tonal; subcut the strip into two 20" backing rectangles.

Step 9. Cut one fusible web piece in each of the following sizes: 1" x 6", 6" x 10" and 10" x 12".

Step 10. Fuse the 1" x 6" piece to black tonal, 6" x 10" piece to the wrong side of the medium red tonal and 10" x 12" piece to dark red tonal.

Step 11. Cut six ⅝" x ¾" M pieces from the fused black tonal.

Step 12. Cut two 1½" x 8½" P and four 1½" x 2⅛" N pieces from the fused medium red tonal.

Step 13. Cut two 3¾" x 8½" O and four 2¼" x 2⅛" L pieces from the fused dark red tonal.

Completing the Snail's Trail Block

Step 1. Sew B to C; press seams toward B. Repeat to make two B-C units.

Step 2. Join the two B-C units to complete the block center as shown in Figure 1; press seam in one direction.

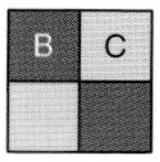

Figure 1

Step 3. Sew D to opposite sides and E to the remaining sides of the block center as shown in Figure 2; press seams toward D and E.

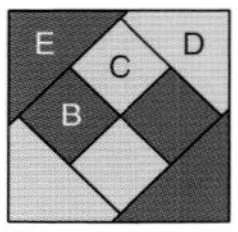

Figure 2

Step 4. Continue adding pieces to the block center in alphabetical order to complete the block as shown in Figure 3, pressing seams away from the block center after each round.

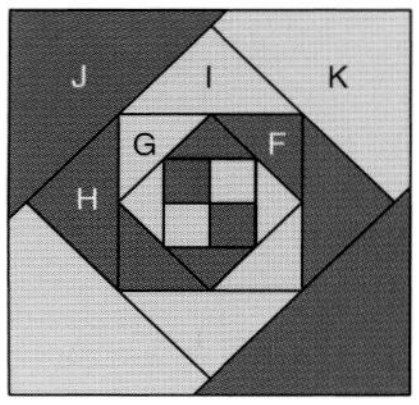

Figure 3

Completing the Cat & Fire Hydrant Blocks

Step 1. Center and fuse a cat shape on one A square. Repeat to fuse two blocks.

Step 2. Center and fuse P on O on the appliqué pressing sheet. ***Note:*** *Remove paper backing from each strip just before fusing.*

Step 3. Move the fused unit to a cutting mat and trim the corners, beginning at the corner of I and angling down 1⅛" on the side edges of O as shown in Figure 4.

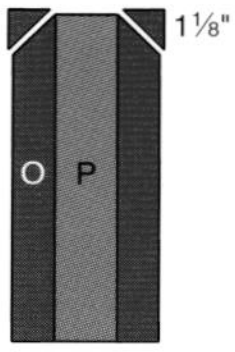

Figure 4

Step 4. Repeat Step 3 with N centered on L, trimming the corners of L ⅜" down on the side edges as shown in Figure 5. Repeat to make two N-L units.

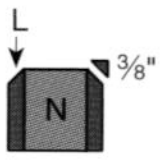

Figure 5

Step 5. Move the fused units back to the appliqué pressing sheet and center the N-L units under the O-P unit 3½" from the bottom of O-P as shown in Figure 6.

Step 6. Center and fuse the ¾"-long side of M under

the top edge and under the two N-L sides of the fused unit, again referring to Figure 6.

Figure 6

Step 7. Pick up the fused unit and center on an A square; fuse in place to complete one Fire Hydrant block. Repeat to make two blocks.

Step 8. Using clear nylon monofilament in the top of the machine and a neutral color all-purpose thread in the bobbin, machine zigzag-stitch fused shapes in place.

Completing the Top

Step 1. Arrange and join the blocks with Q and R triangles in diagonal rows referring to Figure 7; press seams away from the Snail's Trail block and toward Q and R.

Figure 7

Step 2. Join the rows; press seams in one direction.

Step 3. Sew S strips to opposite sides and T strips to the top and bottom of the pieced center; press seams toward S and T.

Step 4. Spray-baste the batting between the lining and the completed top.

Step 5. Quilt as desired by hand or machine; trim edges even.

Step 6. Fold over and press ½" to the wrong side on one 31" edge of each 20" x 31" backing rectangle; fold over another ½" and press. Stitch pressed edges to hem.

Step 7. Lay the quilted top right side up on a flat surface; lay a hemmed backing piece right side down on top, matching raw edges. Pin in place.

Step 8. Referring to Figure 8, lay the second hemmed backing piece on the opposite end of the quilted top, overlapping hemmed edges as necessary; pin and stitch overlap to hold.

Figure 8

Step 9. Stitch all around using a ½" seam allowance; repeat stitching to secure. Zigzag-stitch along raw edges to prevent fraying when in use.

Step 10. Turn cover right side out and insert the pillow form to finish. ❖

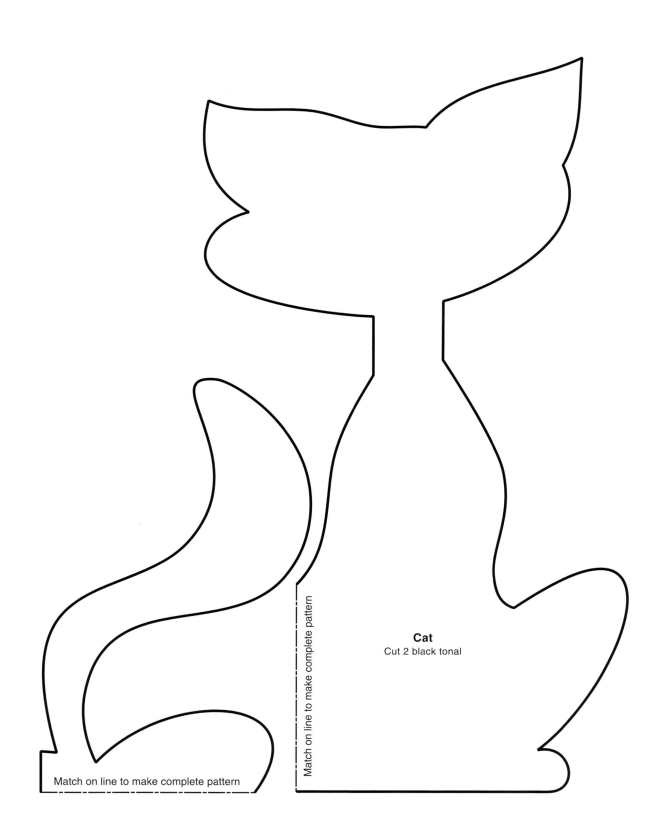

Match on line to make complete pattern

Match on line to make complete pattern

Cat
Cut 2 black tonal

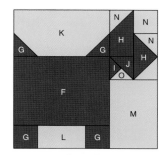

Scottie
12" x 12" Block

Scotties on Parade

Pieced Scotty dogs in bright colors make a perfect quilt for any dog lover.

DESIGN BY LUCY A. FAZELY & MICHAEL L. BURNS

Project Specifications
Skill Level: Intermediate
Quilt Size: 72" x 84"
Block Size: 12" x 12"
Number of Blocks: 15

Materials
- ⅝ yard each pink and very dark purple tonals
- ¾ yard lavender tonal
- ⅞ yard purple tonal
- 1¼ yards each red and blue tonals
- 1½ yards black tonal
- 1⅔ yards dark purple tonal
- Backing 78" x 90"
- Batting 78" x 90"
- All-purpose thread to match fabrics
- Quilting thread
- Basic sewing tools and supplies

Cutting
Step 1. Cut one 12⅞" by fabric width strip each pink (A), purple (B) and lavender (E) tonals; subcut A and E strips into two 12⅞" squares each and the B strip into three 12⅞" squares. Cut each square in half on one diagonal to make four each A and E triangles and six B triangles.

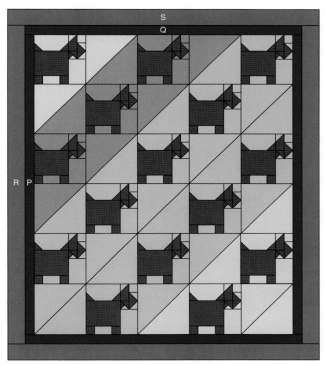

Scotties on Parade
Placement Diagram
72" x 84"

Step 2. Cut two 12⅞" by fabric width strips each blue (C) and red (D) tonals; subcut C strips into five 12⅞" squares and D strips into four 12⅞" squares. Cut each

square in half on one diagonal to make 10 C triangles and eight D triangles.

Step 3. Cut four 6½" by fabric width strips black tonal; subcut strips into (15) 8½" F rectangles.

Step 4. Cut four 2½" by fabric width strips black tonal; subcut strips into (60) 2½" G squares.

Step 5. Cut two 4½" by fabric width strips black tonal; subcut strips into (30) 2½" H rectangles.

Step 6. Cut one 3¼" by fabric width strip black tonal; subcut strip into four 3¼" squares. Cut each square on both diagonals to make 16 I triangles.

Step 7. Cut the remainder of the 3¼" strip to 2⅞" and subcut strip into eight 2⅞" squares. Cut each square in half on one diagonal to make 16 J triangles.

Step 8. Cut one 4½" by fabric width strip pink tonal; subcut strip into one each 8½" K, 6½" M, and 2½" L rectangles, one 3¼" x 3¼" O square and four 2½" x 2½" N squares.

Step 9. Cut one 4½" by fabric width strip lavender tonal; subcut strip into two each 8½" K and 6½" M rectangles and one 3¼" x 3¼" O square.

Step 10. Cut one 2½" by fabric width strip lavender tonal; subcut strip into two 4½" L rectangles and eight 2½" N squares.

Step 11. Cut two 4½" by fabric width strips purple tonal; subcut strips into three each 8½" K and 6½" M rectangles, one 3¼" x 3¼" O square and (12) 2½" x 2½" N squares.

Step 12. Cut one 2½" by fabric width strip purple tonal; subcut strip into three 4½" L rectangles.

Step 13. Cut two 4½" by fabric width strips red tonal; subcut strips into four each 8½" K and 6½" M rectangles and one 3¼" x 3¼" O square.

Step 14. Cut two 2½" by fabric width strips red tonal; subcut strips into four 4½" L rectangles and (16) 2½" N squares.

Step 15. Cut two 4½" by fabric width strips blue tonal; subcut strips into five each 8½" K and 6½" M rectangles and two 3¼" x 3¼" O squares.

Step 16. Cut two 2½" by fabric width strips blue tonal; subcut strips into five 4½" L rectangles and (20) 2½" N squares.

Step 17. Cut seven 2½" by fabric width strips very dark purple tonal. Join strips on short ends to make one long strip; press seams open. Subcut strip into two 72½" P strips and 64½" Q strips.

Step 18. Cut eight 4½" by fabric width strips dark purple tonal. Join strips on short ends to make one long strip; press seams open. Subcut strip into two 76½" R strips and 72½" S strips.

Step 19. Cut eight 2¼" by fabric width strips dark purple tonal for binding.

Completing the Triangle Units

Step 1. Sew A to B along the diagonal to make an A-B triangle unit referring to Figure 1; press seam toward B. Repeat to make two A-B triangle units.

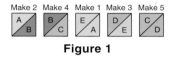

Figure 1

Step 2. Repeat Step 1 to make four B-C, five C-D, three D-E and one A-E unit, again referring to Figure 1; press seams toward darker fabrics.

Completing the Scottie Blocks

Note: *There will be unused A, C, I, J and O triangles when piecing is complete.*

Step 1. Cut each 3¼" x 3¼" O square on both diagonals to make four triangles from each square.

Step 2. To complete one pink Scotty block, select one each F, I and J, two H and four G pieces black solid.

Step 3. Select one each K, L, M and O and four N pieces pink tonal.

Step 4. Draw a diagonal line on the wrong side of two G squares and three N squares.

Step 5. Sew I to O as shown in Figure 2 to make an I-O unit; press seam toward I.

Figure 2    Figure 3

Step 6. Sew J to the I-O unit as shown in Figure 3; press seam toward J.

Step 7. Referring to Figure 4, place an N square on one end of H; stitch on the marked line. Trim seam to ¼" and press N to the right side to complete one H-N unit.

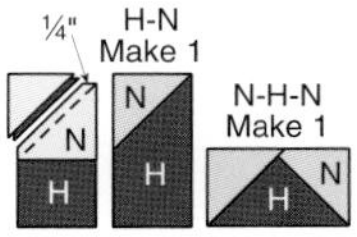

Figure 4

Step 8. Repeat Step 7 with N on both ends of H to complete one N-H-N unit, again referring to Figure 4.

Step 9. Sew the H-N unit to the I-O-J unit as shown in Figure 5; press seam toward H-N.

Figure 5

Step 10. Sew N to the N-H-N unit as shown in Figure 6; press seam toward N.

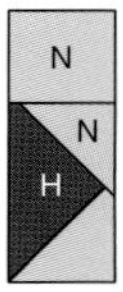

Figure 6

Step 11. Join the two pieced units and add M to complete the head portion of the block as shown in Figure 7; press seam in one direction and toward M.

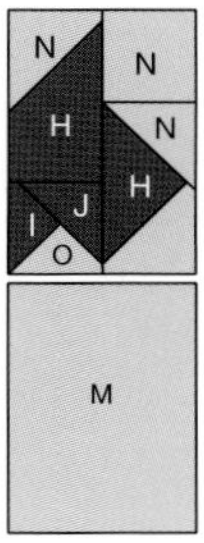

Figure 7

Step 12. Sew G to two opposite ends of K as in Step 8 and as shown in Figure 8 to complete a G-K unit.

Figure 8

Step 13. Sew G to opposite ends of L to complete a G-L unit; press seams toward G.

Step 14. Sew the G-K unit to one side of F and the G-L unit to the opposite side of F to complete the body portion of the block as shown in Figure 9; press seams toward F.

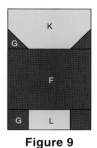

Figure 9

Step 15. Join the head and body sections to complete one pink Scottie block as shown in Figure 10; press seams toward the body section.

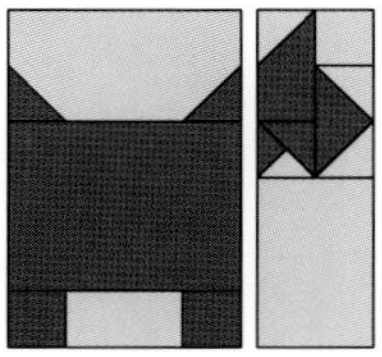

Figure 10

Step 16. Repeat to complete two lavender, three purple, four red and five blue Scottie blocks as shown in Figure 11.

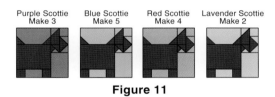

Figure 11

Completing the Quilt

Step 1. Arrange and join the Scottie blocks with the triangle units in rows referring to the Placement Diagram for positioning. Press seams toward triangle units.

Step 2. Join the rows to complete the pieced center; press seams in one direction.

Step 3. Sew P strips to opposite long sides and Q strips to the top and bottom of the pieced center; press seams toward the P and Q strips.

Step 4. Sew R strips to opposite long sides and S strips to the top and bottom to complete the pieced top; press seams toward the R and S strips.

Step 5. Complete the quilt referring to Completing Your Quilt on page 170. ❖

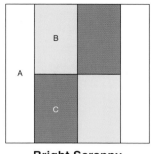

Bright Scrappy
10" x 10" Block

Bright Scrappy Throw

Use up some of those bright prints leftover from other projects to make this quick scrappy quilt, which will add pizzazz to any room.

DESIGN BY RUTH SWASEY

Project Specifications
Skill Level: Beginner
Quilt Size: 70" x 80"
Block Size: 10" x 10"
Number of Blocks: 42

Materials
- ⅝ yard yellow print
- ⅞ yard orange print
- 2¼ yards white multicolored dot
- 3 yards total bright prints
- Backing 76" x 86"
- Batting 76" x 86"
- All-purpose thread to match fabrics
- Quilting thread
- Basic sewing tools and supplies

Cutting
Step 1. Cut six 10½" by fabric width strips white multicolored dot; subcut five strips into (80) 2½" A rectangles. Cut four more 2½" A rectangles from the remaining strip.

Step 2. Subcut the remainder of the 10½" strip into four 2½" x 32" strips for D and E.

Step 3. Cut four 2½" by fabric width strips white multicolored dot. Join these strips on the short ends with the D and E strips cut in Step 2 to make one long strip; press seams open. Subcut strip into two 70½" D strips and two 64½" E strips.

Step 4. Cut (28) 3½" by fabric width B and C strips bright prints.

Step 5. Cut seven 3½" by fabric width strips orange print. Join these strips on the short ends to make one long strip; press seams open. Subcut strip into two 74½" F strips and two 70½" G strips.

Step 6. Cut eight 2¼" by fabric width strips yellow print for binding.

Completing the Blocks
Step 1. Select two different strips bright prints for

B and C. Sew a B strip to a C strip with right sides together along the length; press seam toward darker fabric. Repeat to make 14 B-C strip sets.

Step 2. Subcut the B-C strip sets into (84) 5½" B-C units as shown in Figure 1 to yield 42 pairs of B-C units.

Figure 1

Step 3. To complete one block, select and join two same-fabric B-C units to complete a B-C section as shown in Figure 2; press seam in one direction.

Figure 2

Step 4. Sew an A rectangle to opposite long sides of the B-C section to complete one Bright Scrappy block referring to the block drawing; press seams toward A. Repeat to make 42 blocks.

Completing the Quilt

Step 1. Join six blocks to make a row, alternating the position of the blocks as shown in Figure 3; press seams in one direction. Repeat to make seven rows.

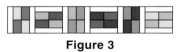

Figure 3

Step 2. Join the rows referring to the Placement Diagram for positioning; press seams in one direction.

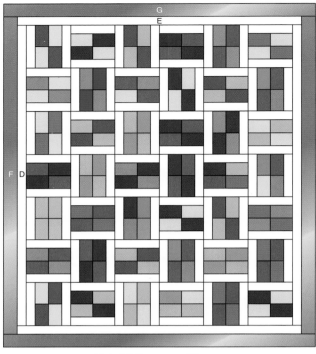

Bright Scrappy Throw
Placement Diagram
70" x 80"

Step 3. Sew D strips to opposite long sides and E strips to the top and bottom of the pieced center; press seams toward D and E strips.

Step 4. Sew F strips to opposite long sides and G strips to the top and bottom of the pieced center to complete the top; press seams toward F and G strips.

Step 5. Complete the quilt referring to Completing Your Quilt on page 170. ❖

Fat Quarter Floral Throw

Create a floral garden with simple strips cut from floral fat quarters.

DESIGN BY CONNIE KAUFFMAN

Project Specifications
Skill Level: Beginner
Quilt Size: 49" x 63"

Materials
- 1 fat quarter each purple, violet and rose florals
- ⅓ yard each yellow, white and peach florals
- ½ yard green mottled
- 2 yards dark green tonal
- Backing 55" x 69"
- Batting 55" x 69"
- All-purpose thread to match fabrics
- Quilting thread
- Basic sewing tools and supplies

Cutting
Step 1. Cut three 4½" by fabric width strips green mottled; subcut strips into (20) 4½" A squares.
Step 2. Cut two 4½" x 16½" B, one 4½" x 5" C and one 4½" x 13½" D strip rose floral.

Step 3. Cut three 4½" x 16½" E, one 4½" x 5" F and one 4½" x 13½" G strip yellow floral.

Step 4. Cut two 4½" x 16½" H, one 4½" x 3" I and one 4½" x 5" J strip violet floral.

Step 5. Cut three 4½" x 16½" K, one 4½" x 13½" L and one 4½" x 7" M strip white floral.

Step 6. Cut three 4½" x 16½" N and one 4½" x 5" O strip purple floral.

Step 7. Cut three 4½" x 16½" P, one 4½" x 13½" Q and one 4½" x 9½" R strip peach floral.

Step 8. Cut six 2¼" by fabric width strips dark green tonal for binding.

Step 9. Cut seven 1½" x 53½" S strips along the length of dark green tonal.

Step 10. Cut two 5½" x 53½" T strips and two 5½" x 49½" U strips along the length of dark green tonal.

Completing the Quilt

Step 1. Arrange and join pieces in rows referring to Figure 1; press seams in one direction.

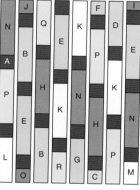

Figure 1

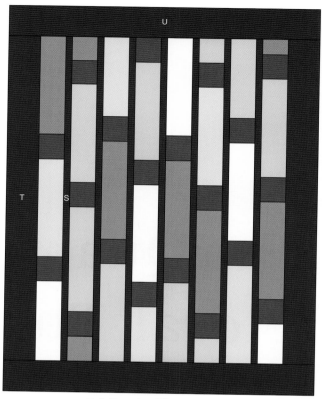

Fat Quarter Floral Throw
Placement Diagram
49" x 63"

Step 2. Join the rows with the S strips referring to the Placement Diagram for positioning; press seams toward S strips.

Step 3. Sew the T strips to opposite long sides and U strips to the top and bottom; press seams toward T and U strips to complete the top.

Step 4. Complete the quilt referring to Completing Your Quilt on page 170. ❖

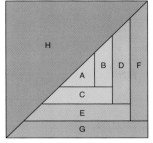

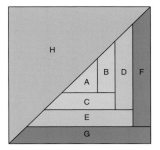

Pink Split Log Cabin
12" x 12" Block
Make 10

Green Split Log Cabin
12" x 12" Block
Make 10

Split Log Cabin

Sherbet colors make this quilt look good enough to eat!

DESIGN BY SANDRA L. HATCH

Project Specifications

Skill Level: Beginner
Quilt Size: 62" x 74"
Block Size: 12" x 12"
Number of Blocks: 20

Materials

- 1 (3⅞") by fabric width strip pink print for A
- ⅓ yard lime green tonal
- ½ yard each pink and green tonals
- ½ yard each pink batik and green with small pink dots
- ⅝ yard each pink with small green dots and medium green tonal
- 1 yard each pink with large green dots and green with large pink dots
- 1 yard pink and green stripe
- Backing 68" x 80"
- Batting 68" x 80"
- All-purpose thread to match fabrics
- Quilting thread
- Basic sewing tools and supplies

Cutting

Step 1. Cut (10) 3⅞" x 3⅞" squares from the 3⅞" pink print A strip; cut each square in half on one diagonal to make 20 A triangles. **Note:** *If you prefer to center a motif in each of these triangles, you may fussy-cut the squares, but you will need more than the one 3⅞" fabric-width strip recommended in the Materials list.*

Step 2. Cut four 2" by fabric width strips each pink and green tonals; subcut each fabric into 10 each 5½" B strips and 7" C strips.

Step 3. Cut two 2½" by fabric width strips each pink and green tonals for M units.

Step 4. Cut five 2" by fabric width strips each pink batik and green with small pink dots; subcut each fabric into 10 each 8½" D strips and 10" E strips.

Step 5. Cut two 2½" by fabric width strips each pink batik and green with small pink dots for M units.

Step 6. Cut seven 2" by fabric width strips each pink with small green dots and medium green tonal; subcut each fabric into 10 each 11¾" F strips and 13¼" G strips.

Step 7. Cut two 2½" by fabric width strips each pink with small green dots and medium green tonal for M units.

Step 8. Cut five 12⅞" x 12⅞" squares each green with large pink dots and pink with large green dots; cut each square in half on one diagonal to make 10 H triangles each fabric.

Step 9. Cut two 2½" by fabric width strips each green with large pink dots and pink with large green dots for M units.

Step 10. Cut six 1½" by fabric width strips lime green tonal. Join strips on short ends to make one long strip; press seams open. Subcut strips into two 60½" I strips and two 50½" J strips.

Step 11. Cut six 2½" by fabric width strips pink-and-green stripe. Join strips on short ends to make one long strip; press seams open. Subcut strips into two 62½" K strips and two 54½" L strips.

Step 12. Cut seven 2¼" by fabric width strips pink-and-green stripe for binding.

Completing the Blocks

Step 1. To make one Pink Split Log Cabin block, select one each pink B–H piece and one A triangle.

Step 2. Sew B to one short edge of A, aligning the square ends as shown in Figure 1; press seam toward B.

Figure 1

Step 3. Repeat Step 2 with C to complete the first round of logs referring to Figure 2; press seam toward C.

Figure 2

Step 4. Continue to add strips to the short sides of A in alphabetical order to complete the pieced triangle as shown in Figure 3.

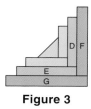

Figure 3

Step 5. Using a straightedge, trim the excess strips even with the edge of the A triangle as shown in Figure 4.

Step 6. Sew an H triangle to the trimmed edge to complete one Pink Split Log Cabin block referring to the block drawing. Repeat to make 10 blocks.

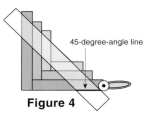

45-degree-angle line

Figure 4

Step 7. Repeat Steps 1–6 with green B–H pieces and A triangles to complete 10 Green Split Log Cabin blocks referring to the block drawing.

Completing the Quilt

Step 1. Join two pink blocks with two green blocks to make an X row as shown in Figure 5; press seams toward the pink blocks. Repeat to make three X rows.

Step 2. Join two green blocks with two pink blocks to make a Y row, again referring to Figure 5; press seams toward the pink blocks. Repeat to make two Y rows.

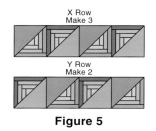

X Row
Make 3

Y Row
Make 2

Figure 5

Step 3. Join the X and Y rows to complete the pieced center referring to the Placement Diagram for positioning of rows; press seams in one direction.

Step 4. Sew an I strip to opposite long sides and J strips to the top and bottom of the pieced center; press seams toward the I and J strips.

Step 5. Sew a K strip to opposite long sides and L strips to the top and bottom of the pieced center; press seams toward the K and L strips.

Step 6. Join one M strip of each fabric color with right sides together along the length to make a strip set; repeat to make two strip sets. Press seams in one direction.

Step 7. Subcut strip sets into (16) 4½" M units as shown in Figure 6.

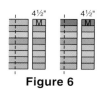

4½"   4½"

Figure 6

Step 8. Join five M units on the short ends in the same color order to make a strip; press seams in one direction. Repeat for two strips. Remove seven pieces from the green end of each strip as shown in Figure 7 to complete two side M strips that begin and end with a pink piece.

Figure 7

Step 9. Sew the side M strips to opposite long sides of the pieced center; press seams toward the K strips.

Step 10. Join three M units as in Step 8 and add a removed section to the pink end to complete the top M strip as shown in Figure 8; press seams in one direction. Repeat to make an identical bottom M strip.

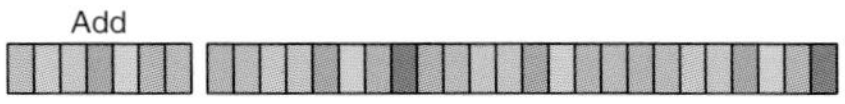

Figure 8

Step 11. Sew the top and bottom M strips to the top and bottom of the pieced center referring to the Placement Diagram for positioning; press seams toward the L strips.

Step 12. Complete the quilt referring to Completing Your Quilt on page 170. ❖

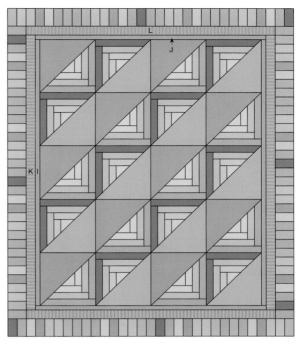

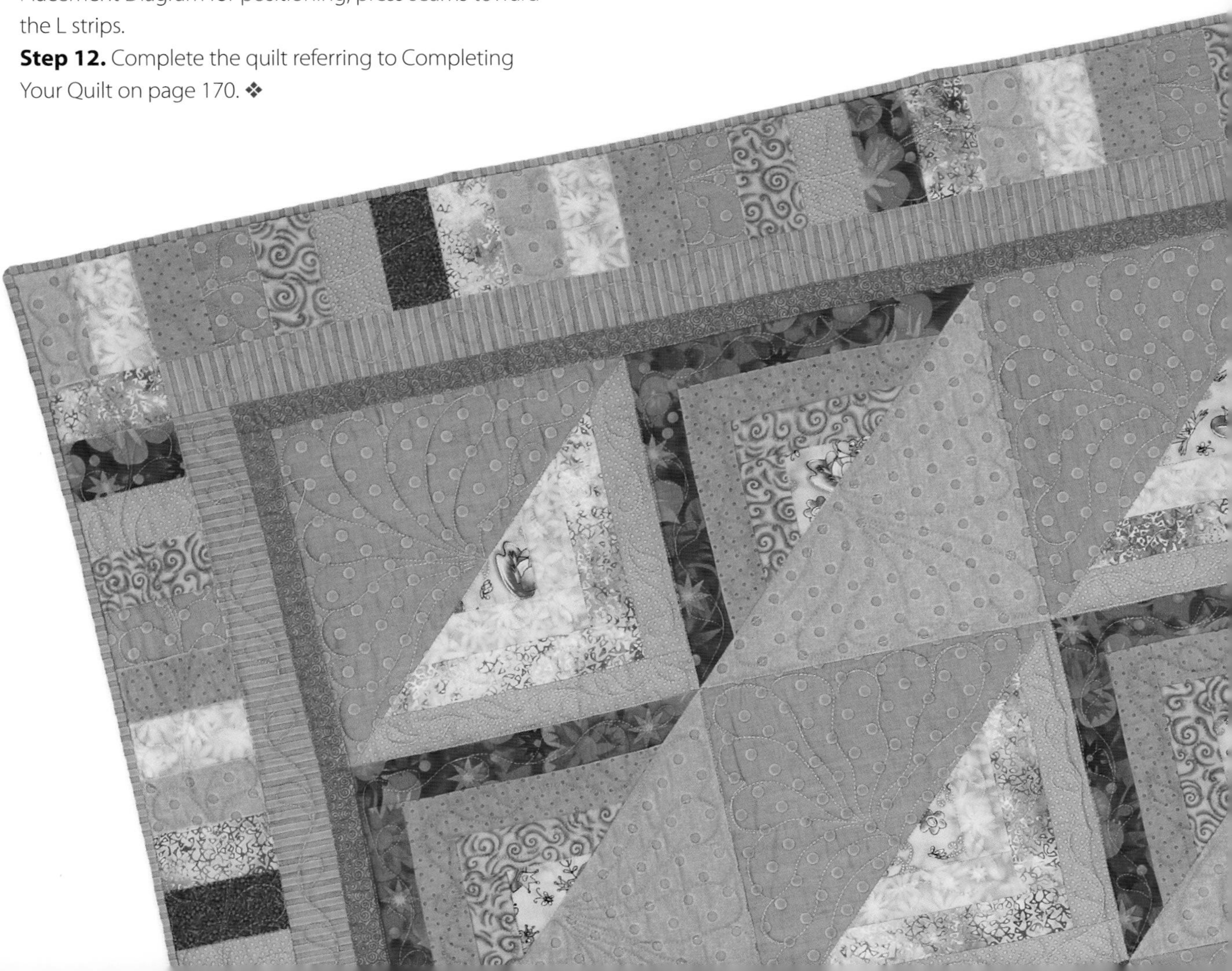

Split Log Cabin
Placement Diagram
62" x 74"

Varsity Rag Quilt

Use up lots of scraps or select a planned color arrangement to make this soft stadium blanket. It will be perfect for a dorm room bed.

DESIGN BY LINDA MILLER

Project Specifications
Skill Level: Beginner
Quilt Size: 66" x 74"

Materials
- ⅝ yard each 14 different fabrics (plush fleece and flannel used in sample)
- 2½ yards border fabric
- 7 yards filler flannel (solid-color diaper flannel)
- All-purpose thread to match fabrics
- Quilting thread
- 56 coordinating buttons in various sizes and shapes
- Sharp scissors or shears
- Basic sewing tools and supplies

Completing the Pieced Center
Note: *Do not prewash fabrics.*
Step 1. Cut a 2¼ yard piece of the filler flannel; set aside to fill border strips.
Step 2. Rip or cut the remaining filler flannel down the fold of the entire length to yield two filler-flannel pieces measuring approximately 22" by 4½ yards.

Step 3. Open up one ⅝-yard fabric piece and place the continuous piece of filler flannel so it fills one side of the ⅝-yard piece as shown in Figure 1. Fold the fabric piece back over the filler flannel to make a fabric sandwich. ***Note:*** *You will be using the continuous piece of filler flannel repeatedly with each ⅝-yard piece.*

Figure 1

Step 4. Cut the fabric sandwich into two 9" strips; subcut each strip into two 9" squares to total four 9"-square fabric sandwiches.
Step 5. Continue to insert the filler flannel into each of the ⅝-yard pieces and cut four 9" x 9" sandwiched squares from each fabric.
Step 6. Lay out the sandwiched squares on a flat surface in eight rows of seven squares each.
Step 7. When satisfied with placement, gather up the sandwiched squares of one row, starting from

the right-hand side, placing square 7 on square 6; continue across the row. Label as row 1. Repeat for all rows.

Step 8. Beginning with row 1, place sandwich 7 on your work surface; place sandwich 6 on top of sandwich 7, matching all edges; join along the right edge using a ½" seam allowance as shown in Figure 2.

Step 9. Pick up the lower left corner of sandwich 6 and "turn the page" referring to Figure 3; repeat Step 8 with sandwich 5 on sandwich 6. Repeat the process to complete the row; repeat for all eight rows.

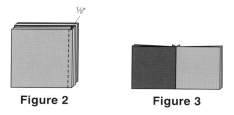

| Figure 2 | Figure 3 |

Step 10. Press seams open.

Step 11. Join the rows in order, matching seams.

Step 12. Stitch a button in the center of each square. *Note: Stitch the buttons on the side with all seam allowances showing.*

Adding Borders

Step 1. Cut (13) 6" by fabric width strips border fabric. Repeat with the 2¼-yard piece of filler flannel.

Step 2. Remove selvage ends from each strip.

Step 3. Join six strips border fabric on the short ends with a ½" seam allowance to make one long strip; repeat to make two long strips.

Step 4. Cut four 57" B strips and four 75" C strips from the border fabric.

Step 5. Insert filler flannel between two B strips, overlapping the filler-flannel edges about ½" and placing the border-strip seam allowance to the inside of the layers. *Note: Overlapping filler flannel instead of joining ends in seams reduces bulk.*

Step 6. Machine-quilt down the center of the layered strips. *Note: The quilt shown used a figure-eight design stitched using a double needle.*

Step 7. Pin and stitch the quilted B strips to the top and bottom of the pieced center, using a ½" seam allowance; press seams open.

Step 8. Repeat Steps 5–7 with C strips, sewing the

strips to opposite long sides of the pieced center; press seams open.

Step 9. Zigzag-stitch ½" from the edges of the quilt all around.

Completing the Quilt

Step 1. Cut close to seam intersections to free the edges for clipping as shown in Figure 4.

Step 2. Cut the intersection layers apart to reduce bulk.

Step 3. Clip seam allowances at ¼" intervals, being careful not to clip into the seam stitches as shown in Figure 5.

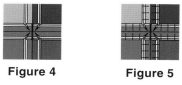

| Figure 4 | Figure 5 |

Step 4. Trim quilt edges even; clip ¼" apart and ¼" deep. Clip corners at a 90-degree angle.

Step 5. Wash and dry the quilt several times using liquid fabric softener to help make the quilt soft and cuddly. *Note: You might want to take the quilt to a Laundromat rather than use your own washer and dryer because of the large amount of lint produced in this process.* ❖

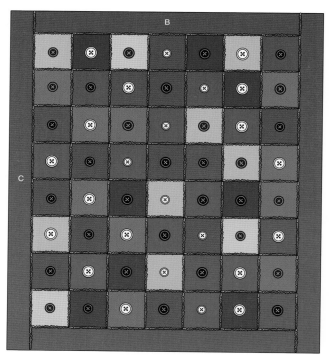

Varsity Rag Quilt
Placement Diagram
66" x 74"

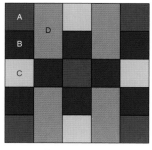

Crossroads
15" x 15" Block

Crossroads

Make a warm flannel quilt this weekend and snuggle in it next week.

DESIGN BY KARLA SCHULZ

Project Specifications
Skill Level: Beginner
Quilt Size: 78" x 108"
Block Size: 15" x 15"
Number of Blocks: 24

Materials
All fabrics are flannel
- 1⅛ yards brown mottled
- 1¾ yards blue print
- 2⅓ yards multicolor print
- 3⅓ yards dark blue mottled
- Backing 84" x 114"
- Batting 84" x 114"
- All-purpose thread to match fabrics
- Quilting thread
- Basic sewing tools and supplies

Cutting
Step 1. Cut (10) 3½" by fabric width A strips brown mottled.
Step 2. Cut (16) 3½" by fabric width B strips dark blue mottled.
Step 3. Cut nine 6½" by fabric width strips dark blue mottled. Join strips on short ends to make one long strip; press seams open. Subcut strips into two 66½" G strips and two 108½" H strips.
Step 4. Cut (16) 3½" by fabric width strips blue print; set aside eight strips for C. Join the remaining strips on short ends to make one long strip; press seams open. Subcut strips into two 60½" E strips and two 96½" F strips.

Step 5. Cut eight 6½" by fabric width D strips multicolor print.

Step 6. Cut (10) 2¾" by fabric width strips multicolor print for binding.

Completing the Blocks

Step 1. Join one C strip with two each A and B strips to make a C strip set referring to Figure 1; press seams away from C. Repeat to make four strip sets.

Step 2. Subcut the C strip sets into (48) 3½" C units, again referring to Figure 1.

Figure 1

Step 3. Sew a B strip between two D strips to make a D strip set referring to Figure 2; press seams toward B. Repeat to make four strip sets.

Figure 2

Step 4. Subcut the D strip sets into (48) 3½" D units, again referring to Figure 2.

Step 5. Join one A strip with two each B and C strips to make an A strip set referring to Figure 3; press seams away from A. Repeat to make two strip sets.

Step 6. Subcut the A strip sets into (24) 3½" A units, again referring to Figure 3.

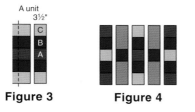

Figure 3   **Figure 4**

Step 7. To complete one Crossroads block, join one A unit with two each C and D units as shown in Figure 4; repeat to make 24 blocks. Press seams in 12 blocks toward the A unit and in the remaining 12 blocks away from the A unit.

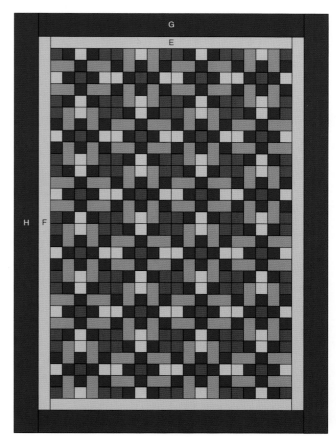

Crossroads
Placement Diagram
78" x 108"

Completing the Quilt

Step 1. Join four blocks with seams pressed toward the A unit to make a row, alternating the position of the blocks; press seams in one direction. Repeat to make three rows.

Step 2. Repeat Step 1 with four blocks with seams pressed away from the A unit to make a row; press seams in the opposite direction of the previously stitched rows.

Step 3. Join the rows, alternating the pressing directions, to complete the pieced top; press seams in one direction.

Step 4. Sew an E strip to the top and bottom and F strips to opposite sides of the pieced center; press seams toward E and F strips.

Step 5. Sew a G strip to the top and bottom and H strips to opposite sides of the pieced center; press seams toward G and H strips to complete the pieced top.

Step 6. Complete the quilt referring to Completing Your Quilt on page 170. ❖

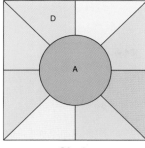

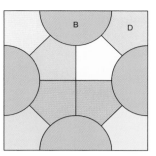

Circle
12" x 12" Block
Make 12

Half-Circle
12" x 12" Block
Make 18

New Moon Throw

Use up lots of scraps to make this unusual quilt.

DESIGN BY RUTH SWASEY

Project Specifications
Skill Level: Intermediate
Quilt Size: 66" x 78"
Block Size: 12" x 12"
Number of Blocks: 30

Materials
- 1¼ yards dark pink floral for A circles and borders
- 2⅛ yards pink print for B and C pieces and binding
- 4 yards total light scraps for D triangles
- Backing 72" x 84"
- Batting 72" x 84"
- All-purpose thread to match fabrics
- Quilting thread
- 4½ yards fusible web
- Basic sewing tools and supplies

Cutting
Step 1. Prepare templates for A–C using pattern pieces given. Trace shapes onto the paper side of the fusible web as directed on each piece for number to cut.
Step 2. Cut out shapes, leaving a margin around each one. Fuse shapes to the wrong side of fabrics as directed on each piece for color and number to cut.
Step 3. Cut out shapes on traced lines; remove paper backing.

New Moon Throw
Placement Diagram
66" x 78"

Step 4. Cut (120) 6⅞" x 6⅞" D squares light scraps; mark a diagonal line from corner to corner on 60 D squares.
Step 5. Cut seven 3½" by fabric width strips dark pink floral. Join the strips on the short ends to make one long strip; press seams open. Subcut strips into two 72½" E strips and two 66½" F strips.
Step 6. Cut eight 2¼" by fabric width strips pink print for binding.

Completing the Circle Blocks

Step 1. Place one unmarked D square right sides together with a marked D square.
Step 2. Referring to Figure 1, sew ¼" on each side of the marked line.

Figure 1

Step 3. Cut the stitched unit apart on the marked line to make two D units as shown in Figure 2. Repeat to make 120 D units; set aside 72 D units to make Half-Circle blocks.

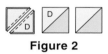

Figure 2

Step 4. To complete one Circle block, join two D units to make a row as shown in Figure 3; press seam in one direction. Repeat to make two rows.

Figure 3

Step 5. Join the rows to complete the D background referring to Figure 4; press seam in one direction.

Figure 4

Step 6. Center and fuse an A circle on the center of the D background to complete one block referring to the block drawing; repeat to make 12 Circle blocks.

Completing the Half-Circle Blocks

Step 1. To complete one Half-Circle block, repeat Steps

4 and 5 for Completing the Circle blocks referring to Figure 5 for positioning of D pieces when joining.

Figure 5

Step 2. Center and fuse B to each side edge of the D background to complete one block referring to the block drawing; repeat to make 18 Half-Circle blocks.

Completing the Quilt

Step 1. Join six Half-Circle blocks to make a vertical X row referring to Figure 6; repeat to make three rows. Press seams in one direction.

Figure 6

Step 2. Join six Circle blocks to make a vertical Y row, again referring to Figure 6; repeat to make two rows. Press seams in one direction.
Step 3. Arrange and fuse a C piece to the corners of each top and bottom block in each Y row as shown in Figure 7.

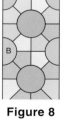

Figure 7   **Figure 8**

Step 4. Arrange and fuse B pieces over the seam between the blocks on each edge of the Y rows as shown in Figure 8.
Step 5. Using thread to match fabrics, straight-stitch close to the edges of each fused shape to secure.

Step 6. Join the rows to complete the pieced center referring to the Placement Diagram for positioning of rows; press seams in one direction.

Step 7. Sew E strips to opposite long sides and F strips to the top and bottom of the pieced center; press seams toward the E and F strips.

Step 8. Complete the quilt referring to Completing Your Quilt on page 170. ❖

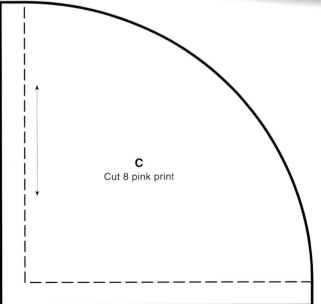

C
Cut 8 pink print

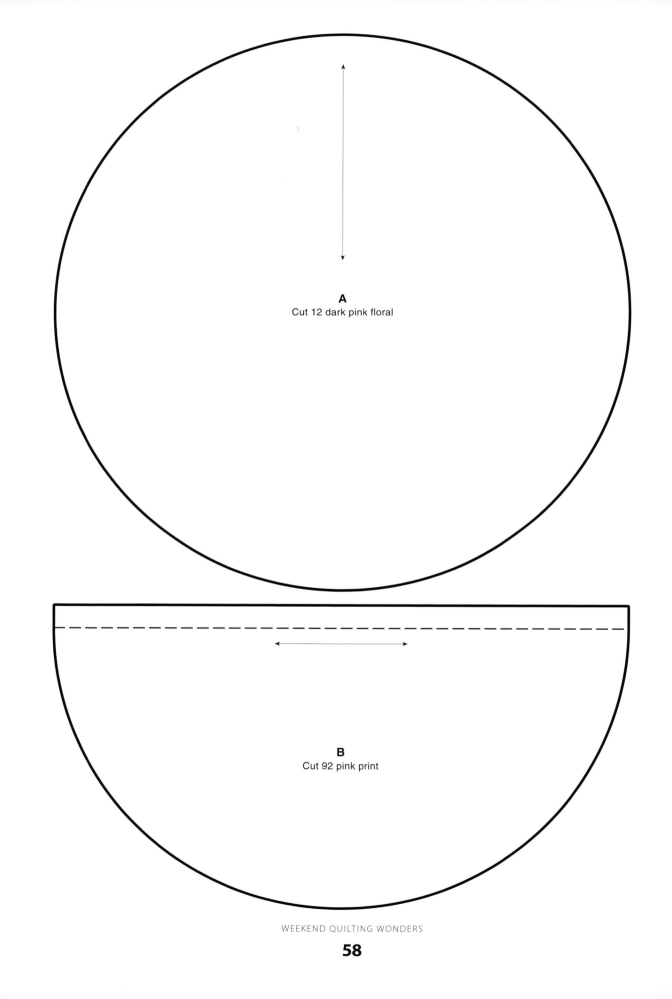

A
Cut 12 dark pink floral

B
Cut 92 pink print

Summer Garden

Complementary colors blue and yellow make a perfect summer runner.

DESIGN BY TOBY LISCHKO

Project Specifications
Skill Level: Beginner
Runner Size: 54" x 27"

Materials
- ⅜ yard yellow floral
- ¾ yard yellow print
- 1 yard blue print
- 1⅜ yards blue floral
- Backing 56" x 29"
- Batting 56" x 29"
- All-purpose thread to match fabrics
- Quilting thread
- Basic sewing tools and supplies

Cutting
Step 1. Cut one 9½" by fabric width strip yellow floral; subcut strip into four 9½" A squares.

Step 2. Cut two 5" by fabric width strips blue print; subcut strips into (16) 5" B squares. Draw a diagonal line from corner to corner on the wrong side of each square.

Step 3. Cut two 9½" by fabric width strips blue print; subcut strips into (10) 5" C pieces.

Step 4. Cut three 5" by fabric width strips yellow print; subcut strips into (20) 5" D squares. Mark a

diagonal line from corner to corner on the wrong side of each square.

Step 5. Cut two 5" x 45½" H strips and two 5" x 18½" G strips along the length of the blue floral.

Step 6. Cut two 5⅜" x 5⅜" squares each yellow print (F) and four squares blue floral (E); cut each square in half on one diagonal to make four F and eight E triangles.

Completing the Units

Step 1. Referring to Figure 1, stitch B along the marked line to opposite corners of A; trim seams to ¼" and press B to the right side. Repeat on the remaining corners of A to complete an A-B unit. Repeat to make four A-B units.

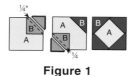

Figure 1

Step 2. Referring to Figure 2, stitch D to one end of C; trim seam to ¼" and press D to the right side. Repeat on the opposite end of C to complete a C-D unit. Repeat to make 10 C-D units.

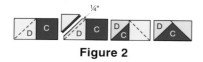

Figure 2

Step 3. Sew E to F along the diagonal; press seam toward E. Repeat to make four E-F units.

Completing the Runner

Step 1. Join four A-B units with two C-D units to make the center row as shown in Figure 3; press seams in one direction.

Figure 3

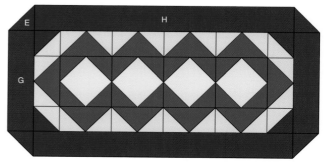

Summer Garden
Placement Diagram
54" x 27"

Step 2. Join four C-D units with two E-F units to make the top row as shown in Figure 4; press seams in the opposite direction from the center row. Repeat to make the bottom row.

Figure 4

Step 3. Join the rows to complete the pieced center; press seams toward the center row.

Step 4. Sew H strips to opposite long sides of the pieced center; press seams toward H strips.

Step 5. Sew E to each end of each G strip; press seams toward E. Repeat to make two E-G strips.

Step 6. Sew the E-G strips to each short end of the pieced center referring to the Placement Diagram for positioning; press seams toward the E-G strips to complete the runner top.

Step 7. Lay the batting on a flat surface; place the backing right side up on the batting. Place the pieced top right sides together with the layered batting and backing; smooth and pin to hold.

Step 8. Sew all around the outside edges, leaving a 6" opening on one side. Trim backing even with top and batting close to stitching.

Step 9. Turn right side out through the opening; press opening seams under ¼"; hand-stitch opening closed.

Step 10. Quilt as desired by hand or machine to finish. ❖

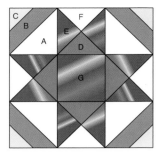

Flower Power
12" x 12" Block

Flower Power

Bright colors make this a fun quilt for all generations.

DESIGN BY JULIE WEAVER

Project Specifications
Skill Level: Beginner
Quilt Size: 51" x 63"
Block Size: 12" x 12"
Number of Blocks: 12

Materials
- ⅓ yard white/purple dot
- ¾ yard purple tonal
- ⅞ yard white/pink dot
- 1¼ yards pink tonal
- 1⅔ yards purple print
- Backing 57" x 69"
- Batting 57" x 69"
- All-purpose thread to match fabrics
- Quilting thread
- Basic sewing tools and supplies

Cutting
Step 1. Cut three 4⅞" by fabric width strips each white/pink dot (A) and purple tonal (B); subcut strips into (24) 4⅞" squares each fabric. Draw a diagonal line from corner to corner on the wrong side of each A square.
Step 2. Cut one 6" by fabric width strip purple tonal; subcut strip into four 6" O squares. Cut eight 1½" x 1½" J squares from the remainder of the strip.

Step 3. Cut three 2½" by fabric width strips white/purple dot; subcut strips into (48) 2½" C squares. Draw a diagonal line from corner to corner on the wrong side of each square.
Step 4. Cut two 5¼" by fabric width strips each pink tonal (D) and white/pink dot (F); subcut strips into (12) 5¼" squares each fabric.
Step 5. Cut (10) 1½" by fabric width strips pink tonal. Join strips on short ends to make one long strip; press seams open. Subcut strips into two 48½" H strips, two 36½" I strips, two 61½" M strips and two 49½" N strips.
Step 6. Cut six 2¼" by fabric width strips pink tonal for binding.
Step 7. Cut two 4½" by fabric width strips purple print; subcut strips into (12) 4½" G squares.
Step 8. Cut three 5¼" by fabric width strips purple print; subcut strips into (24) 5¼" E squares.
Step 9. Cut five 6" by fabric width strips purple print. Join strips on short ends to make one long strip; press seams open. Subcut strip into two 50½" K strips and two 38½" L strips.

Completing the Blocks
Step 1. Draw a diagonal line from corner to corner on the wrong side of each E square.
Step 2. Place an E square right sides together with the

D and F squares; sew ¼" on each side of the marked line as shown in Figure 1.

Figure 1

Step 3. Cut apart on the drawn line; open and press seam toward E as shown in Figure 2.

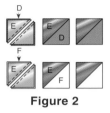

Figure 2

Step 4. Draw a diagonal line from corner to corner on the wrong side of each E-D unit.

Step 5. Place an E-D unit right sides together with an E-F unit and stitch ¼" on each side of the marked line as shown in Figure 3.

Figure 3

Step 6. Cut the stitched unit apart on the marked line to make two D-E-F units as shown in Figure 4; repeat to make 48 units.

Figure 4

Step 7. Place an A square right sides together with a B square; stitch ¼" on each side of the marked line as shown in Figure 5. Repeat with all A and B squares.

Figure 5

Step 8. Cut a stitched unit apart on the marked line to make two A-B units as shown in Figure 6; repeat to make 48 units.

Figure 6

Step 9. Place a C square right sides together on the B corner of one A-B unit and stitch on the marked line as shown in Figure 7.

Figure 7

Step 10. Trim seam to ¼" and press C to the right side to complete an A-B-C unit; repeat to make 48 units.

Step 11. To complete one Flower Power block, join two A-B-C units with one D-E-F unit to make the top row as shown in Figure 8; press seams toward the A-B-C units. Repeat to make the bottom row.

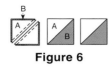

Figure 8

Step 12. Sew a D-E-F unit to opposite sides of G to make the center row as shown in Figure 9; press seams toward G.

Figure 9

Step 13. Sew the top and bottom rows to the center row referring to the block drawing to complete one block; press seams toward the center row; repeat to make 12 blocks, pressing seams in half the blocks away from the center row.

Completing the Quilt

Step 1. Join three blocks to make a row; press seams in one direction; repeat to make four rows.

Step 2. Join the rows, alternating the direction of the pressed seams, to complete the pieced center; press seams in one direction.

Step 3. Sew an H strip to opposite long sides of the pieced center; press seams toward H strips.

Step 4. Sew J to each end of each I strip; press seams toward I strips.

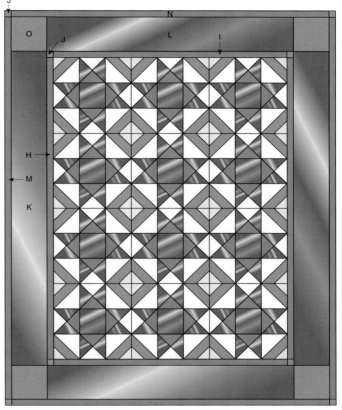

Flower Power
Placement Diagram
51" x 63"

Step 5. Sew an I-J strip to the top and bottom of the pieced center; press seams toward the I-J strips.

Step 6. Sew a K strip to opposite long sides of the pieced center; press seams toward K strips.

Step 7. Sew an O square to each end of each L strip; press seams toward L strips.

Step 8. Sew an L-O strip to the top and bottom of the pieced center; press seams toward the L-O strips.

Step 9. Sew an M strip to opposite long sides of the pieced center; press seams toward M strips.

Step 10. Sew a J square to each end of each N strip; press seams toward N strips.

Step 11. Sew a J-N strip to the top and bottom of the pieced center to complete the pieced top; press seams toward the J-N strips.

Step 12. Complete the quilt referring to Completing Your Quilt on page 170. ❖

Flower
8" x 8" Block
Make 24

Leaf
8" x 8" Block
Make 8

Garden Breeze

Paper-pieced flowers create a fabric garden in this pretty throw.

DESIGN BY RHONDA L. TAYLOR

Project Specifications
Skill Level: Intermediate
Quilt Size: 45" x 71"
Block Size: 8" x 8"
Number of Blocks: 32

Materials
- ⅜ yard red metallic dot
- ⅝ yard gold print
- ⅝ yard dark green tonal
- 1 yard red/black print
- 2 yards black floral
- 2¼ yards light green tonal
- Backing 51" x 77"
- Batting 51" x 77"
- All-purpose thread to match fabrics
- Quilting thread
- Basic sewing tools and supplies

Cutting
Step 1. Make one copy of the paper-piecing patterns given; join the two sections of each pattern to make two complete patterns. Make copies of the complete patterns as directed.
Step 2. Using the cut paper patterns, cut 24 fabric pieces of each Flower block piece and eight of each Leaf block piece as directed on paper-piecing patterns for color, adding ½" all around. **Note:** *These pieces do not have to be perfect; they have to be larger than the template, but any excess is trimmed away after stitching.*
Step 3. Cut four 1" by fabric width strips red metallic dot. Join two strips on the short ends to make one long strip; press seams open. Repeat. Subcut one 64½" A strip from each joined strip.
Step 4. Cut two 1" x 33½" B strips red metallic dot.
Step 5. Cut four 6½" by fabric width strips black floral. Join two strips on the short ends to make one long strip; press seams open. Repeat. Subcut one 65½" C strip from each joined strip.

> ### Tip
> Fold the paper toward you on the sewing line and trim excess fabric for seam allowance. This makes removing the paper later easier.
>
> Lightweight sew-in interfacing may be used instead of paper. It does not have to be removed. Wash-away fabric stabilizer will work also. The completed quilt top should be placed in water to remove the stabilizer before quilting.

Step 6. Cut three 3½" by fabric width strips black floral. Join the strips on the short ends to make one long strip; press seams open. Subcut strip into two 45½" D strips.

Step 7. Cut six 2¼" by fabric width strips gold print for binding.

Completing the Blocks

Step 1. Set your machine to a small stitch length to make paper removal easier later.

Step 2. Select a flower paper-piecing pattern. Place fabric to cover area 1 on paper pattern with wrong side of fabric against the unmarked side of the paper, allowing fabric to extend at least ¼" into adjacent areas as shown in Figure 1.

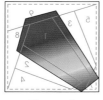

Figure 1

Step 3. Place fabric for area 2 right sides together with fabric 1 on the 1-2 edge as shown in Figure 2; pin along the 1-2 line. Fold fabric 2 over to cover area 2, allowing fabric to extend at least ¼" into adjacent areas as shown in Figure 3. Adjust fabric if necessary. Unfold fabric 2 to lie flat on fabric 1; pin in place. **Note:** *Check that each piece will cover its area before stitching.*

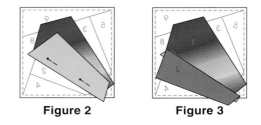

Figure 2   **Figure 3**

Step 4. Flip paper pattern; stitch on the 1-2 line beginning and ending 2 or 3 stitches into adjacent areas. **Note:** *On edge pieces, stitch to the outside edge of the pattern.*

Step 5. Trim the 1-2 seam allowance to ⅛"–¼" as shown in Figure 4. Fold fabric 2 to cover area 2; lightly press with a warm dry iron.

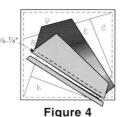

⅛–¼"

Figure 4

Step 6. Continue to add fabric pieces in numerical order to cover the paper pattern as shown in Figure 5.

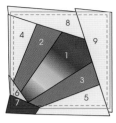

Figure 5

Step 7. Pin outside fabric edges to paper pattern. Trim paper and fabric edges even on the outside heavy solid line as shown in Figure 6 to complete one Flower block. Repeat all steps to complete 24 Flower blocks and eight Leaf blocks.

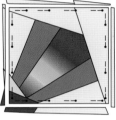

Figure 6

Completing the Quilt

Step 1. Join four Flower blocks to make an X row as shown in Figure 7; press seams in one direction. Repeat to make four X rows.

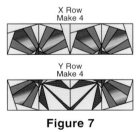

X Row
Make 4

Y Row
Make 4

Figure 7

Step 2. Join two Leaf blocks and two Flower blocks to make a Y row, again referring to Figure 7; press seams in the opposite direction from the X rows. Repeat to make four Y rows.

Step 3. Join the rows to complete the pieced center

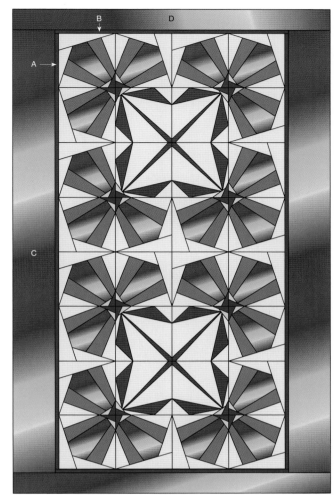

Garden Breeze
Placement Diagram
45" x 71"

referring to the Placement Diagram for positioning; press seams in one direction.

Step 4. Sew A strips to opposite long sides and B strips to the top and bottom of the pieced center; press seams toward A and B strips.

Step 5. Sew C strips to opposite long sides and D strips to the top and bottom of the pieced center; press seams toward C and D strips.

Step 6. Remove paper patterns.

Step 7. Complete the quilt referring to Completing Your Quilt on page 170. ❖

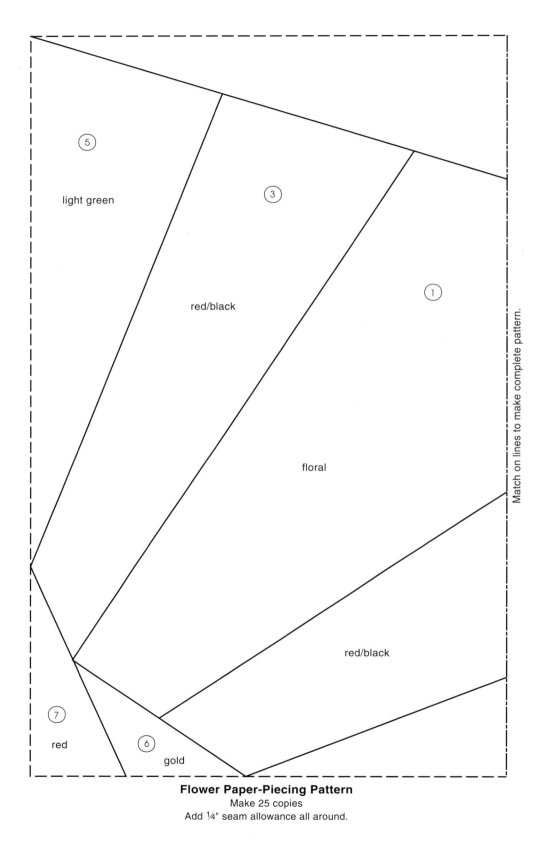

Match on lines to make complete pattern.

⑤ light green

③ red/black

① floral

① red/black

⑦ red

⑥ gold

Flower Paper-Piecing Pattern
Make 25 copies
Add ¼" seam allowance all around.

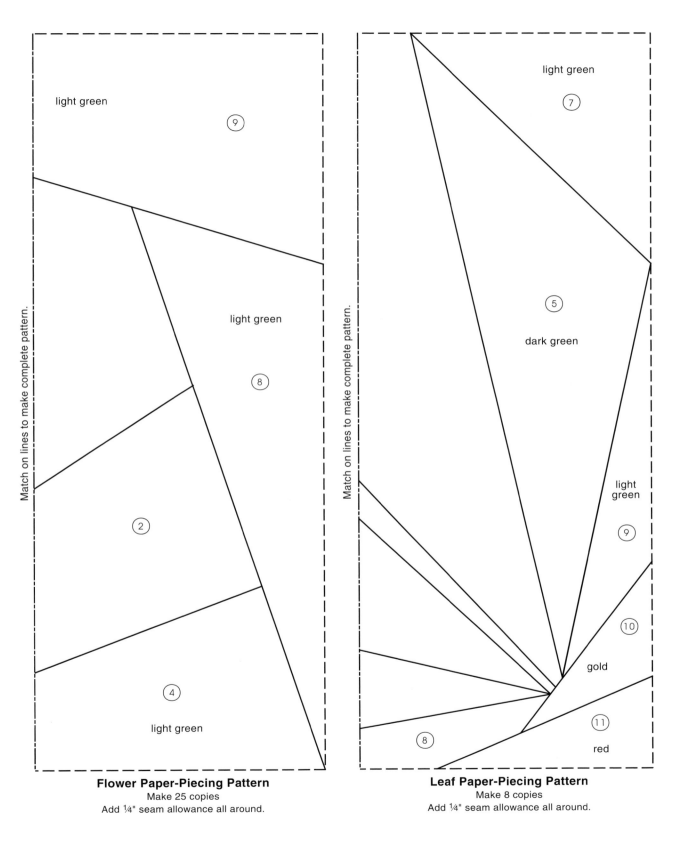

Flower Paper-Piecing Pattern
Make 25 copies
Add ¼" seam allowance all around.

Leaf Paper-Piecing Pattern
Make 8 copies
Add ¼" seam allowance all around.

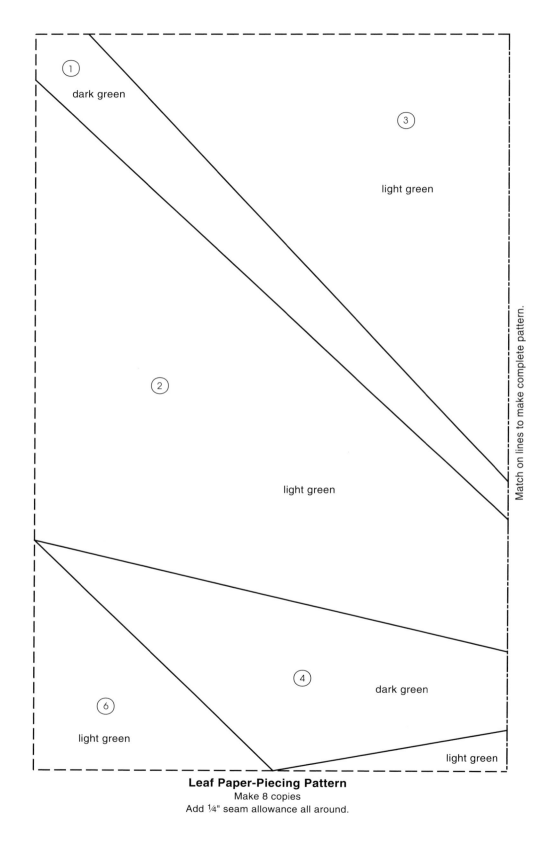

① dark green

③ light green

② light green

light green

④ dark green

⑥ light green

light green

Match on lines to make complete pattern.

Leaf Paper-Piecing Pattern
Make 8 copies
Add ¼" seam allowance all around.

Square
6" x 6" Block
Make 50

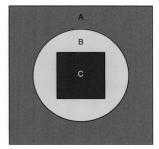

Circle
6" x 6" Block
Make 50

Circles & Squares

A Polynesian look is created using bright red and yellow batiks.

DESIGN BY RUTH SWASEY

Project Specifications
Skill Level: Beginner
Quilt Size: 64" x 64"
Block Size: 6" x 6"
Number of Blocks: 100

Materials
- 1½ yards yellow batik
- 1¾ yards red/yellow batik
- 2⅝ yards navy batik
- Backing 70" x 70"
- Batting 70" x 70"
- All-purpose thread to match fabrics
- Quilting thread
- 2¼ yards 18"-wide fusible web
- Basic sewing tools and supplies

Cutting
Step 1. Cut nine 6½" by fabric width strips red/yellow batik; subcut strips into (50) 6½" A squares.
Step 2. Cut (11) 2½" by fabric width strips yellow batik. Set aside four strips for D. Join the remaining seven strips on short ends to make one long strip; press seams open. Subcut strip into two 60½" G strips and two 64½" H strips.

Step 3. Bond fusible web to the wrong side of a 22" by fabric width piece of the yellow batik. Prepare a template for B using pattern given; trace 50 B circles onto the paper side of the fused fabric. Cut out shapes on traced lines; remove paper backing.

Step 4. Cut a 7" by fabric width strip navy batik; bond fusible web to the wrong side.

Step 5. Cut three 2" by fabric width strips from the fused navy batik; subcut strips into (50) 2" C squares. Remove paper backing.

Step 6. Cut eight 2½" by fabric width E strips navy batik.

Step 7. Cut seven 6½" by fabric width strips navy batik; subcut strips into (100) 2½" F pieces.

Step 8. Cut seven 2¼" by fabric width strips navy batik for binding.

Completing the Circle Blocks

Step 1. Fold each A and C square and the B circle in quarters and crease to mark the centers.

Step 2. To complete one block, center C on B; fuse in place.

Step 3. Center the B-C unit on A; fuse in place to complete one block. Repeat to make 50 Circle blocks.

Completing the Square Blocks

Step 1. Sew a D strip between two E strips with right sides together along the length; press seams toward E strips. Repeat to make four D-E strip sets.

Step 2. Subcut strip sets into (50) 2½" D-E units as shown in Figure 1.

Figure 1

Step 3. Sew F to each side of a D-E unit to complete one block referring to the block drawing; press seams toward F. Repeat to make 50 Square blocks.

Completing the Quilt

Step 1. Join five each Circle and Square blocks to make a row, alternating blocks; press seams toward Circle blocks. Repeat to make 10 rows.

Step 2. Join the rows referring to the Placement Diagram for positioning; press seams in one direction.

Step 3. Sew G strips to opposite sides and H strips to the remaining sides to complete the pieced top; press seams toward G and H strips.

Step 4. Complete the quilt referring to Completing Your Quilt on page 170. ❖

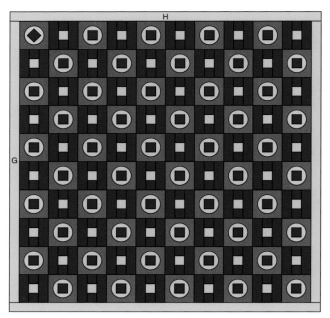

Circles & Squares
Placement Diagram
64" x 64"

B
Cut 50 yellow batik

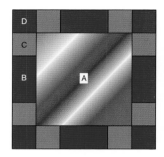

Quilter's Delight
12" x 12" Block

Quilter's Delight

A sewing novelty print is featured in the center of the blocks in this easy-to-stitch bed quilt. Any novelty print will work in this setting.

DESIGN BY SANDRA L. HATCH

Project Specifications
Skill Level: Beginner
Quilt Size: 81" x 95"
Block Size: 12" x 12"
Number of Blocks: 20

Materials
- ⅞ yard blue print
- 1⅛ yards sewing print
- 1¼ yards tan tonal
- 1⅝ yards coordinating stripe
- 1⅝ yards green print
- 2⅔ yards burgundy tonal
- Backing 87" x 101"
- Batting 87" x 101"
- All-purpose thread to match fabrics
- Quilting thread
- Basic sewing tools and supplies

Cutting
Step 1. Cut four 8½" by fabric width strips sewing print; subcut strips into (20) 8½" A squares.
Step 2. Cut six 4½" by fabric width B strips burgundy tonal.

Step 3. Cut six 2½" by fabric width D strips burgundy tonal.
Step 4. Cut nine 2¼" by fabric width strips burgundy tonal for binding.
Step 5. Cut seven 3" by fabric width strips burgundy tonal. Join strips on short ends to make one long strip; press seams open. Subcut strip into two 74½" I strips and two 65½" J strips.
Step 6. Cut four 6½" x 6½" M squares burgundy tonal.
Step 7. Cut (12) 2½" by fabric width C strips tan tonal.
Step 8. Cut seven 1½" by fabric width strips tan tonal. Join strips on short ends to make one long strip; press seams open. Subcut strip into two 72½" G strips and two 60½" H strips.
Step 9. Cut nine 2½" by fabric width E strips blue print; subcut four of the strips into (52) 2½" E squares. Set aside remaining five strips for E-F units.
Step 10. Cut (10) 5½" by fabric width F strips green print.
Step 11. Cut eight 6½" by fabric width strips coordinating stripe. Join strips on short ends to make one long strip, matching as necessary to make a continuous stripe pattern; press seams open. Subcut strip into two 83½" K and two 69½" L strips.

Completing the Blocks

Step 1. Sew a B strip between two C strips with right sides together along the length; press seams toward B. Repeat to make six strip sets.

Step 2. Subcut three of the strip sets into (40) 2½" B-C units as shown in Figure 1.

Figure 1

Step 3. Sew a D strip to each long side of each of the remaining three B-C strip sets; press seams toward D.

Step 4. Subcut the B-C-D strip sets into (40) 2½" B-C-D units, again referring to Figure 1.

Step 5. To complete one block, sew a B-C unit to opposite sides of A; press seams toward A. Add a B-C-D unit to the remaining sides referring to the block drawing to complete the block; press seams toward the B-C-D units. Repeat to make 20 blocks.

Completing the Quilt

Step 1. Sew an E strip between two F strips with right sides together along the length; press seams toward F strips. Repeat to make five strip sets.

Step 2. Subcut the E-F strip sets into (71) 2½" E-F units as shown in Figure 2.

Figure 2

Step 3. Join four blocks with five E-F units to complete a block row; press seams toward the E-F units. Repeat to make five block rows.

Step 4. Join four E-F units with five E squares to complete a sashing row; press seams toward the E-F units. Repeat to make six sashing rows.

Step 5. Join the block rows with the sashing rows to complete the pieced center; press seams toward the sashing rows.

Step 6. Sew G strips to opposite long sides and H strips to the top and bottom of the pieced center; press seams toward G and H strips.

Step 7. Sew I strips to opposite long sides and J strips to the top and bottom of the pieced center; press seams toward I and J strips.

Step 8. Join six E-F units with six E squares to make a strip; press seams toward E. Repeat to make two long E-F strips. Remove one F segment from one end of each strip as shown in Figure 3. Cut a 2½" x 2½" square from each removed F segment.

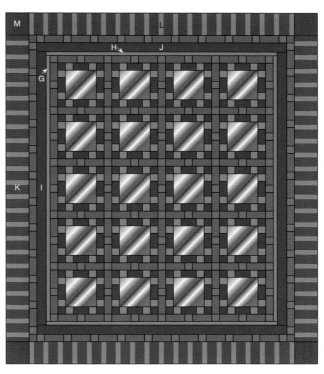

Quilter's Delight
Placement Diagram
81" x 95"

Figure 3

Step 9. Join five E-F units with five E squares to make a strip; press seams toward E. Repeat to make two short E-F strips. Trim the E-F end of each strip to make the F piece 2¼" long referring to Figure 4. Add a trimmed 2½" x 2½" square from Step 8 to the E end of each strip, again referring to Figure 4.

Trim to 2¼"   Add 2½"

Figure 4

Step 10. Sew a long E-F strip to the long sides of the pieced center; press seams toward the I strips.

Step 11. Sew a short E-F strip to the top and bottom; press seams toward J strips.

Step 12. Sew K strips to opposite long sides of the pieced center; press seams toward the K strips.

Step 13. Sew an M square to each end of each L strip; press seams toward L.

Step 14. Sew the L-M strips to the top and bottom of the pieced center to complete the top; press seams toward the L-M strips.

Step 15. Complete the quilt referring to Completing Your Quilt on page 170. ❖

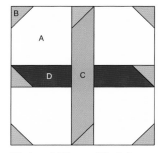

Stained Glass Christmas
16" x 16" Block

Stained Glass Christmas

Pieced units create a stained glass look in this simple bed-size quilt.

DESIGN BY RHONDA TAYLOR

Project Specifications
Skill Level: Beginner
Quilt Size: 73" x 105"
Block Size: 16" x 16"
Number of Blocks: 24

Materials
- 1 yard red tonal
- 1⅛ yards lavender print
- 1¼ yards purple plaid
- 2⅛ yards gold tonal
- 4⅛ yards cream plaid
- Backing 79" x 111"
- Batting 79" x 111"
- All-purpose thread to match fabrics
- Quilting thread
- Basic sewing tools and supplies

Cutting
Step 1. Cut (20) 7¼" by fabric width strips cream plaid; subcut strips into (96) 7¼" A squares.

Step 2. Cut (14) 3" by fabric width strips gold tonal; subcut strips into (192) 3" B squares. Draw a diagonal line from corner to corner on the wrong side of each square.

Step 3. Cut eight 1" by fabric width strips gold tonal. Join strips on short ends to make one long strip; press seams open. Subcut strips into two 96½" E strips and two 65½" F strips.

Step 4. Cut nine 2¼" by fabric width strips gold tonal for binding.

Step 5. Cut two 16½" by fabric width strips lavender print; subcut strips into (24) 3" C strips.

Step 6. Cut four 7¼" by fabric width strips red tonal; subcut strips into (48) 3" D rectangles.

Step 7. Cut nine 4½" by fabric width strips purple plaid. Join strips on short ends to make one long strip; press seams open. Subcut strips into two 97½" G strips and two 73½" H strips.

Completing the Blocks
Step 1. Referring to Figure 1, place a B square on

one corner of A; stitch on the marked line. Trim seam to ¼"; press B to the right side to complete an A-B unit. Repeat to make 96 A-B units.

Figure 1

Step 2. Repeat Step 1 with B and D to make 48 B-D units and with two B squares and C to make 48 B-C units referring to Figure 2.

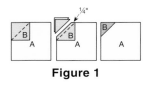

Figure 2

Step 3. To complete one block, join two A-B units with a B-D unit as shown in Figure 3; press seams toward the A-B unit. Repeat to make two A-B-D rows.

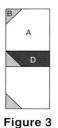

Figure 3

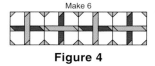

Stained Glass Christmas
Placement Diagram
73" x 105"

Step 4. Join the two A-B-D rows with the B-C unit referring to the block drawing to complete one block; press seams toward the B-C units. Repeat to make 24 blocks.

Completing the Quilt

Step 1. Join four blocks to make a row referring to Figure 4; press seams in one direction. Repeat to make six rows.

Make 6

Figure 4

Step 2. Join the rows to complete the pieced center referring to the Placement Diagram for positioning; press seams in one direction.

Step 3. Sew an E strip to opposite long sides and F strips to the top and bottom of the pieced center; press seams toward E and F strips.

Step 4. Sew G strips to opposite long sides and H strips to the top and bottom of the pieced center; press seams toward G and H strips to complete the top.

Step 5. Complete the quilt referring to Completing Your Quilt on page 170. ❖

Christmas Ribbons

Strips sets and framed squares make up the rows in this fast and easy holiday quilt, which will brighten any bedroom.

DESIGN BY CONNIE RAND

Project Specifications
Skill Level: Beginner
Quilt Size: 84" x 99"

Materials
- ¾ yard red print
- ¾ yard green print
- 1⅓ yards holly print
- 2 yards gold tonal
- 2 yards black print
- 3 yards poinsettia print
- Backing 90" x 105"
- Batting 90" x 105"
- All-purpose thread to match fabrics
- Quilting thread
- Basic sewing tools and supplies

Cutting
Step 1. Cut three 5½" by fabric width strips poinsettia print; subcut strips into (20) 5½" A squares.
Step 2. Cut two 8½" x 83½" L strips and two 8½" x 84½" M strips along the remaining length of the poinsettia print.

Step 3. Cut two 5½" by fabric width strips black print; subcut strips into (40) 1¾" B strips.
Step 4. Cut two 8" by fabric width strips black print; subcut strips into (40) 1¾" C strips.
Step 5. Cut eight 2½" by fabric width strips black print. Join strips on short ends to make one long strip; press seams open. Subcut strips into two 79½" J strips and two 68½" K strips.
Step 6. Cut nine 2¼" by fabric width strips black print for binding.
Step 7. Cut five 4¼" by fabric width strips each red (F) and green (G) prints; subcut two 4¼" F squares from one F strip and two 4¼" G squares from one G strip.
Step 8. Cut (27) 1¾" by fabric width D strips gold tonal.
Step 9. Cut seven 2½" by fabric width strips gold tonal. Join strips on short ends to make one long strip; press seams open. Subcut strip into two 75½" H strips and two 64½" I strips.
Step 10. Cut (18) 2⅜" by fabric width E strips holly print.

Piecing the Units
Step 1. Sew a B strip to opposite sides of each A square; press seams toward B strips.

Step 2. Sew a C strip to the top and bottom of each A-B unit to complete 20 A-B-C units as shown in Figure 1; press seams toward C strips.

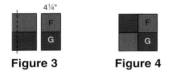 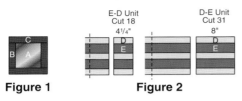

Figure 1   **Figure 2**

Step 3. Join two E strips with three D strips with right sides together along the length to make a D-E strip set as shown in Figure 2; press seams toward the E strips. Repeat to make nine strip sets.

Step 4. Subcut strip sets into (18) 4¼" E-D units and (31) 8" D-E units, again referring to Figure 2.

Step 5. Sew an F strip to a G strip with right sides together along the length to make an F-G strip set; press seams toward G. Repeat to make five F-G strip sets.

Step 6. Subcut the F-G strip sets into (38) 4¼" F-G units as shown in Figure 3.

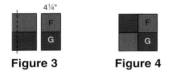

Figure 3   **Figure 4**

Step 7. Join two F-G units to make a Four-Patch unit as shown in Figure 4; press seam in one direction. Repeat to make 12 Four-Patch units.

Completing the Quilt

Step 1. Join one each F and G squares with three F-G units and four E-D units to make an X row referring to Figure 5; press seams away from the E-D units. Repeat to make two X rows.

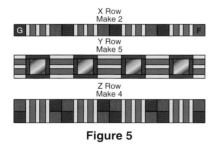

X Row
Make 2

Y Row
Make 5

Z Row
Make 4

Figure 5

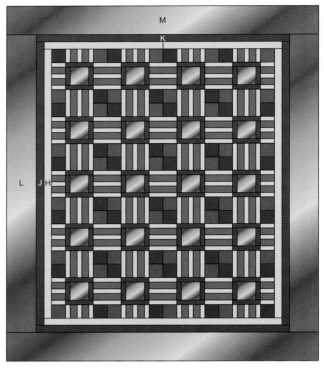

Christmas Ribbons
Placement Diagram
84" x 99"

Step 2. Join two E-D units with three D-E units and four A-B-C units to make a Y row, again referring to Figure 5; press seams away from the D-E and E-D units. Repeat to make five Y rows.

Step 3. Join two F-G units with three Four-Patch units and four D-E units to make a Z row, again referring to Figure 5; press seams away from the D-E units. Repeat to make four Z rows.

Step 4. Join the rows referring to the Placement Diagram for positioning; press seams toward the Y rows.

Step 5. Sew H strips to opposite long sides and I strips to the top and bottom of the pieced center; press seams toward the H and I strips.

Step 6. Sew J strips to opposite long sides and K strips to the top and bottom of the pieced center; press seams toward the J and K strips.

Step 7. Sew L strips to opposite long sides and M strips to the top and bottom of the pieced center; press seams toward the L and M strips.

Step 8. Complete the quilt referring to Completing Your Quilt on page 170. ❖

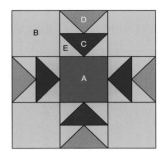

Mardi Gras Christmas
9" x 9" Block

Mardi Gras Christmas

Bright yellow combines with red and green to make a fun and unique

Christmas quilt with a festive flavor. It's time to celebrate!

DESIGN BY LUCY A. FAZELY & MICHAEL L. BURNS

Project Specifications

Skill Level: Beginner
Quilt Size: 50¼" x 63"
Block Size: 9" x 9"
Number of Blocks: 18

Materials

- ½ yard medium and dark red mottleds
- ½ yard dark green mottled
- 1½ yards medium green mottled
- 2¼ yards gold mottled
- Backing 56" x 69"
- Batting 56" x 69"
- All-purpose thread to match fabrics
- Quilting thread
- Basic sewing tools and supplies

Cutting

Step 1. Cut two 3½" by fabric width strips medium green mottled; subcut strips into (18) 3½" A squares.

Step 2. Cut six 4½" by fabric width strips medium green mottled. Join strips on short ends to make one long strip; press seams open. Subcut strips into two 55½" J strips and two 50¾" K strips.

Step 3. Cut six 2¼" by fabric width strips medium green mottled for binding.

Step 4. Cut six 3½" by fabric width strips gold mottled; subcut strips into (72) 3½" B squares.

Step 5. Cut (14) 2" by fabric width strips gold mottled; subcut strips into (288) 2" E squares. Draw a diagonal line from corner to corner on the wrong side of each E square.

Step 6. Cut two 7¼" x 7¼" squares gold mottled; cut each square in half on one diagonal to make four F triangles.

Step 7. Cut one 14" by fabric width strip gold mottled; subcut strip into three 14" squares. Cut each square on both diagonals to make 12 G triangles; discard two triangles.

Step 8. Cut four 3½" by fabric width strips each dark red (C) and medium red (D) mottleds; subcut strips into (72) 2" rectangles each fabric.

Step 9. Cut five 2½" by fabric width strips dark green mottled. Join strips on short ends to make one long strip; press seams open. Subcut strip into two 51½" H strips and two 42¾" I strips.

Completing the Blocks

Step 1. Referring to Figure 1, sew E to one end of C on the marked line; trim seam to ¼" and press E to the right side. Repeat on the opposite end of C to complete a C-E unit; repeat to make 72 C-E units.

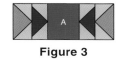

Figure 1

Step 2. Repeat Step 1 to make 72 D-E units, again referring to Figure 1.

Step 3. To complete one Mardi Gras block, sew a C-E unit to a D-E unit to make a side unit as shown in Figure 2; press seam toward the C-E unit. Repeat to make four side units.

Figure 2   **Figure 3**

Step 4. Sew a side unit to opposite sides of A to make the center row as shown in Figure 3; press seams toward A.

Step 5. Sew B to opposite sides of a side unit to complete the top row as shown in Figure 4; press seams toward B. Repeat to make the bottom row.

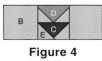

Figure 4

Step 6. Sew the center row between the top and bottom rows to complete one block referring to the block drawing; press seams away from the center row. Repeat to make 18 blocks.

Completing the Quilt

Step 1. Arrange the blocks in diagonal rows with F and G referring to Figure 5; join blocks in diagonal rows. Press seams toward F and G and in one direction.

Figure 5

Step 2. Join the pieced diagonal rows to complete the pieced center; press seams in one direction.

Step 3. Sew H strips to opposite long sides and I strips to the top and bottom of the pieced center; press seams toward H and I strips.

Step 4. Sew J strips to opposite long sides and K strips to the top and bottom of the pieced center; press seams toward J and K strips to complete the pieced top.

Step 5. Complete the quilt referring to Completing Your Quilt on page 170. ❖

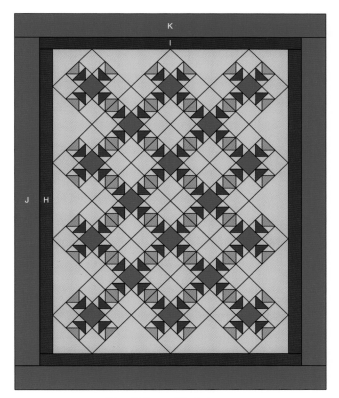

Mardi Gras Christmas
Placement Diagram
50¼" x 63"

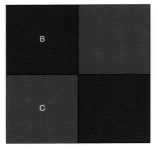

Red/Green Four-Patch
4" x 4" Block
Make 24

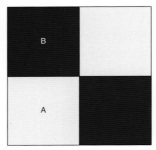

Green Four-Patch
4" x 4" Block
Make 2

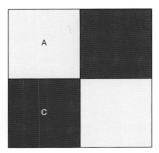

Red Four-Patch
4" x 4" Block
Make 2

Holiday Triangles

Simple Four-Patch units in different sizes are framed with triangles to make a unique table topper that fits any size of table.

DESIGN BY SANDRA L. HATCH

Project Specifications
Skill Level: Beginner
Quilt Size: 44" x 44" without side triangles
Block Size: 4" x 4"
Number of Blocks: 28

Materials
- ¾ yard cream tonal
- 1¼ yards dark green tonal
- 1 yard Christmas floral
- 1½ yards red print
- Backing 50" x 50"
- Batting 50" x 50"
- 2 (15" x 15") squares lightweight batting
- All-purpose thread to match fabrics
- Quilting thread
- Basic sewing tools and supplies

Cutting
Step 1. Cut one 2½" by fabric width A strip cream tonal; cut the strip in half to make two 21½" A strips.
Step 2. Cut three 4½" by fabric width strips cream tonal; subcut strips into (16) 4½" G squares and four 8½" D rectangles.
Step 3. Cut four 4⅞" x 4⅞" squares cream tonal; cut each square in half on one diagonal to make eight J triangles.
Step 4. Cut four 2½" by fabric width strips each dark green tonal (B) and red print (C). Cut one B strip and one C strip in half to make two each 21" B and C strips. Set aside one half-strip each for another project.
Step 5. Cut two 2½" x 32½" H strips and two 2½" x 36½" I strips red print.
Step 6. Cut five 2¼" by fabric width strips red print for binding.
Step 7. Cut two 15" x 15" squares each Christmas floral (L) and red print; cut each square in half on one diagonal to make four each L and backing triangles.
Step 8. Cut two 8½" by fabric width strips Christmas floral; subcut strips into four 16½" E rectangles.
Step 9. Cut two 8½" by fabric width strips dark green tonal; subcut strips into eight 8½" F squares. Draw a diagonal line from corner to corner on the wrong side of each square.

Step 10. Cut two 12⅞" x 12⅞" squares dark green tonal; cut each square in half on one diagonal to make four K triangles.

Completing the Blocks

Step 1. Sew a half-A strip to a half-B strip with right sides together along the length; press seams toward the B strip.

Step 2. Subcut the A-B half-strip set into four 2½" A-B units as shown in Figure 1.

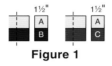

Figure 1

Step 3. Join two A-B units to make a Green Four-Patch block as shown in Figure 2; press seam in one direction. Repeat to make two blocks.

Figure 2

Step 4. Repeat Steps 1 and 2 with one half-A strip and one half-C strip to make four 2½" A-C units, again referring to Figure 1.

Step 5. Join two A-C units to make a Red Four-Patch block, again referring to Figure 2; press seam in one direction. Repeat to make two blocks.

Step 6. Sew a B strip to a C strip with right sides together along the length; press seams toward B strips. Repeat to make three B-C strip sets.

Step 7. Subcut the B-C strip sets into (48) 2½" B-C units referring to Figure 3.

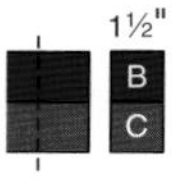

Figure 3

Step 8. Join two B-C units to make a Red/Green Four-Patch block as shown in Figure 4; press seam in one direction. Repeat to make 24 blocks.

Figure 4

Completing the Quilt

Step 1. Sew a Green Four-Patch block to a Red Four-Patch block to make a row as shown in Figure 5; press seam in one direction. Repeat to make two rows.

Figure 5

Step 2. Join the two rows to complete the center Four-Patch unit as shown in Figure 6; press seam in one direction.

Figure 6

Step 3. Sew D to opposite sides of the center Four-Patch unit; press seams toward D.

Step 4. Sew a Red/Green Four-Patch block to each end of each remaining D to make the top and bottom rows as shown in Figure 7; press seams toward D.

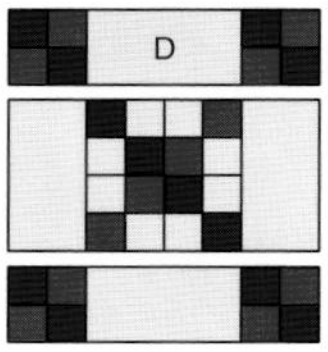

Figure 7

Step 5. Sew the rows to the top and bottom of the stitched D/center unit, again referring to Figure 7.

Step 6. Referring to Figure 8, place an F square right sides together on one end of E and stitch on the marked line. Trim seam to ¼" and press F to the right side.

Figure 8

Step 7. Repeat Step 6 on the remaining end of E to complete an E-F unit, again referring to Figure 8; repeat to make four E-F units.

Step 8. Sew G to a Red/Green Four-Patch block to make a row as shown in Figure 9; press seams toward G. Repeat to make eight rows. Join two rows to complete a corner unit as shown in Figure 10; press seam in one direction. Repeat to make four corner units.

Figure 9

Figure 10

Step 9. Sew an E-F unit to opposite sides of the pieced center unit as shown in Figure 11; press seams toward E-F units.

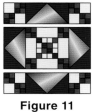

Figure 11

Step 10. Sew a corner unit to opposite ends of each remaining E-F unit and sew to the remaining sides of the pieced center, again referring to Figure 11. Press seams toward the E-F units.

Step 11. Sew an H strip to opposite sides and I strips to the top and bottom of the pieced unit; press seams toward the H and I strips.

Step 12. Join three Red/Green Four-Patch blocks with two G squares and two J triangles to make a side strip as shown in Figure 12; press seams toward G and J. Repeat to make four side strips.

Figure 12

Step 13. Center and sew a side strip to each side of the pieced center as shown in Figure 13. **Note:** *The side strips do not extend to each end of the pieced center.*

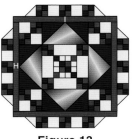

Figure 13

Step 14. Align a straightedge with the edges of J at each corner and trim excess H and I strips as shown in Figure 14, leaving ¼" seam allowance beyond the corner of the G squares.

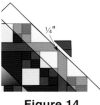

Figure 14

Step 15. Sew a K triangle to each trimmed corner to complete the pieced top.

Step 16. Prepare for quilting and quilt referring to Completing Your Quilt on page 170.

Step 17. Cut each 15" x 15" batting square in half on one diagonal to make four batting triangles.

Step 18. Place a batting triangle on a flat surface; place a red print backing triangle right side up on the batting triangle. Place an L triangle right sides together with the layered batting and backing; pin to hold.

Step 19. Stitch around the short sides of the layered triangles, leaving the long edge open; trim batting close to seam and turn right side out. Press flat. Repeat to make four triangle units.

Step 20. Quilt the triangle units as desired.

Step 21. Center and pin a quilted triangle right sides together between the K triangles on each side of the pieced and quilted top as shown in Figure 15; machine-baste to hold in place.

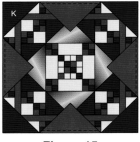

Figure 15

Step 22. Bind edges of quilt referring to Completing Your Quilt on page 170.

Figure 16

Step 23. After binding has been stitched in place on the back side of the quilt, press the quilted L triangles to the right side and topstitch ¼" from the binding seam to finish as shown in Figure 16. ❖

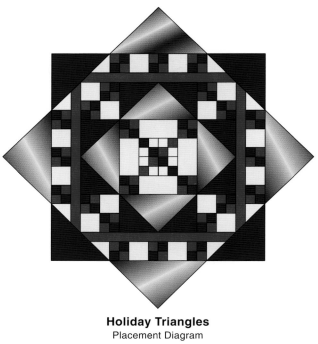

Holiday Triangles
Placement Diagram
44" x 44" without side triangles

Circle the Tree

Only two shapes are used in the six sections of this pretty holiday tree skirt.

DESIGN BY LUCY A. FAZELY & MICHAEL L. BURNS

Project Specifications
Skill Level: Intermediate
Tree Skirt Size: 46" x 39¾"

Materials
- ⅓ yard each medium and dark red tonals
- ⅝ yard each light and medium green tonals
- 1 yard dark green tonal
- Backing 52" x 46"
- Batting 52" x 46"
- All-purpose thread to match fabrics
- Quilting thread
- Basting spray
- Basic sewing tools and supplies

Cutting
Step 1. Prepare templates using pattern pieces given; use templates to cut pieces from strips cut in the following steps.
Step 2. Cut two 8½" by fabric width strips each medium and dark green tonals; cut 12 A pieces from each color.

Step 3. Cut one 8½" by fabric width strip each medium and dark red tonals; cut six A pieces from each strip.
Step 4. Cut five 2½" by fabric width strips dark green tonal for binding.
Step 5. Cut two 7½" by fabric width strips light green tonal; cut 18 B pieces from the strips.

Completing the Tree Skirt
Step 1. Sew a dark red A to a medium red A to a dark green A to complete a red A unit as shown in Figure 1; press seams away from the center A. Repeat to complete six red A units.

Figure 1

Step 2. Sew a dark green A between two medium green A pieces to complete a green A unit, again referring to Figure 1; press seams toward the center A. Repeat to complete six green A units.
Step 3. Sew one red A unit to one green A unit as shown in Figure 2; press seam in one direction.

Figure 2

Step 4. Sew B to the red/red side and both green/green sides of the A unit to complete an A-B unit as shown in Figure 3. Repeat to make six A-B units.

Figure 3

Step 5. Join the A-B units as shown in Figure 4; press seams in one direction.

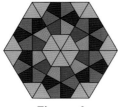

Figure 4

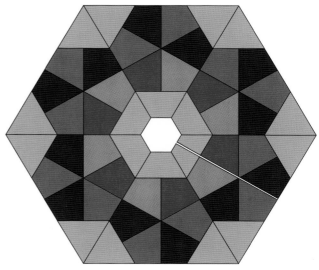

Circle the Tree
Placement Diagram
46" x 39¾"

Step 6. Layer and quilt referring to Completing Your Quilt on page 170.
Step 7. Cut an opening from the outside edge to the center through all layers. Trim away the center B points to 4" from the A-B seams to make the center opening as shown in Figure 5.

Figure 5

Step 8. Bind the edges of the tree skirt with previously cut binding strips to finish referring to Completing Your Quilt on page 170. ❖

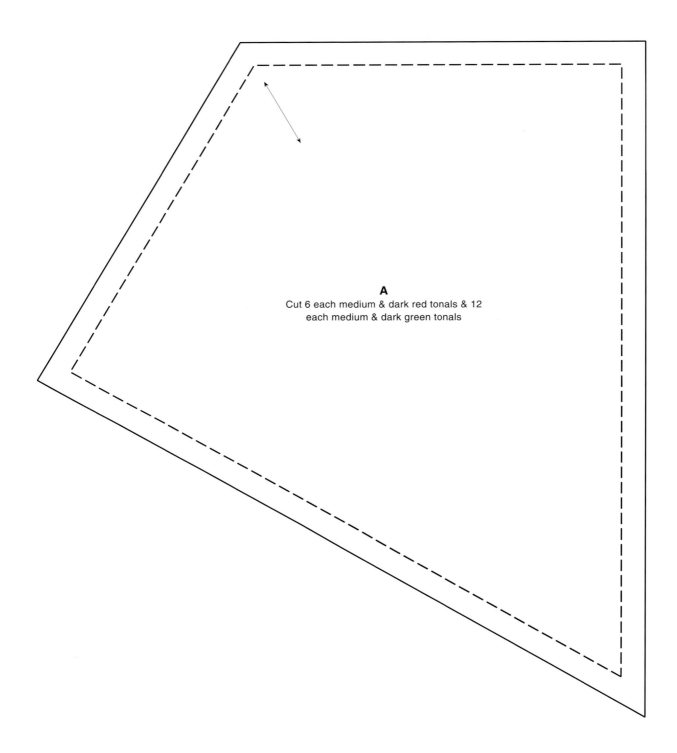

A
Cut 6 each medium & dark red tonals & 12
each medium & dark green tonals

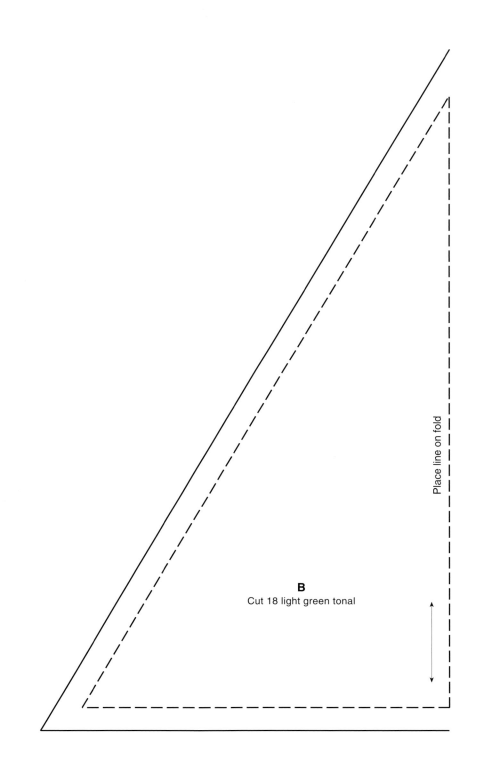

B
Cut 18 light green tonal

Place line on fold

Festive Squares Stocking

Make an elegant Christmas stocking using decorator fabrics.

DESIGN BY SANDEE WINROW MILHOUSE

Project Specifications
Skill Level: Intermediate
Stocking Size: 12½" x 21"

Materials
- 3" x 6" scrap copper decorator fabric
- ¼ yard each taupe, rust and dark olive decorator fabrics
- ¾ yard sage-green decorator fabric
- ¾ yard olive lining fabric
- ¾ yard pre-quilted olive/copper fabric
- 15" x 24" fusible fleece
- All-purpose thread to match fabrics
- Quilting thread
- ½ yard 22"-wide lightweight fusible interfacing
- ⅛ yard 18"-wide fusible web
- Basic sewing tools and supplies

Making Stocking Body
Step 1. Trace and cut out the stocking pattern given following instructions on pattern pieces to make a complete full-size pattern. **Note:** *The C-C connecting line must taper slightly to fit.*

Step 2. Cut one stocking from fusible fleece with fusible side up for left-facing toe.

Step 3. Fuse the fleece stocking to the wrong side of the pre-quilted fabric referring to the manufacturer's instructions. **Note:** *To reduce bulk, use fusible interfacing instead of fleece. If using interfacing, you will need an additional ½ yard of interfacing and no fusible fleece.*

Step 4. Cut out stocking following the shape of the fleece leaving a generous ¾" around the fusible-fleece stocking shape.

Step 5. Pin stocking shape right sides together on the pre-quilted fabric; cut out a second piece for the stocking back.

Step 6. Lay the two pre-quilted stocking pieces (still pinned with right sides together) onto the lining fabric layers (also right sides together); pin all four layers together with the fusible-fleece layer on the top; cut out stocking shape. **Note:** *You may baste the*

layers together, stitching just outside of the fusible fleece, using it as a guide for stitching.

Step 7. Stitch (or serge) the four layers together, leaving top edge unstitched, stitching just outside of the fusible fleece, using it as a guide for stitching.

Step 8. Trim the top of the stocking, leaving ½" above the fusible fleece.

Step 9. Trim other edges to approximately ¼" around stitching.

Step 10. Turn stocking section right side out with lining inside and baste shell and lining pieces together ¼" from the top edge; set stocking aside.

Making the Cuff

Step 1. Cut three 5" x 8½" pieces fusible interfacing; fuse a piece to the wrong side of taupe (T), dark olive (O) and rust (R). Fuse a 5" x 13" strip of fusible interfacing to the wrong side of sage green (G).

Step 2. Cut one 3⅞" x 4⅛" rectangle each G, O and R from the interfaced strip.

Step 3. Cut one 3⅞" x 3⅞" square each O and R and two 3⅞" x 3⅞" squares each G and T from the interfaced strip.

Step 4. Fuse a 2" x 5" strip of fusible web to sage green (G), copper (C) and rust (R). Cut three 1⅛" x 1⅛" squares each fabric.

Step 5. Arrange the interfaced squares to make two rows and the 3⅞" x 4⅛" rectangles to make the top row as shown in Figure 1.

Figure 1

Step 6. Join the pieces in rows; press seams open.

Step 7. Join the three rows, matching seams; press seams open.

Step 8. Mark the top edge of the cuff on the back side for future reference.

Step 9. Center a small fused square on each piece of the pieced section as shown in Figure 2; fuse in place.

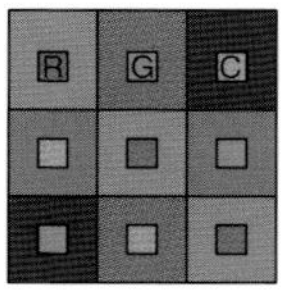

Figure 2

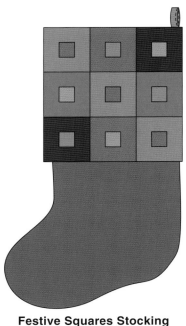

Festive Squares Stocking
Placement Diagram
12½" x 21"

Step 10. Zigzag-stitch around the edges of each square using thread to match fabrics.

Step 11. Place the completed cuff unit on the sage green fabric with right sides together; cut out a lining piece slightly larger than the cuff unit.

Step 12. Stitch along the bottom edge of the cuff unit through both layers; press seam toward the lining piece. Fold lining to the back of the cuff unit to complete the cuff front.

Step 13. Baste side edges ⅛" from edge of the cuff unit; trim excess lining piece even with the edges of the cuff front. ***Note:*** *The piece should now measure 10⅝" x 10⅝".*

Step 14. Cut a 10⅝" x 21¼" sage green rectangle; fold the 21¼" side in half with wrong sides together to form a 10⅝" square; press folded edge to make cuff back.

Step 15. Pin the cuff front right sides together with the cuff back, aligning the finished end of the front with the folded end of the back; stitch left and right edge together using a ¼" seam allowance. Turn right side out; press.

Step 16. Baste around the top edge of the cuff to hold the lining and outer layer together.

Making Hanging Loop

Step 1. Cut a 2" x 5" piece of sage green. Fold the long raw edge in ½" to meet in the center as shown in Figure 3; press.

Figure 3

Step 2. Fold the pressed pieces in half along length again; press and stitch to make a ½" x 5" strip, again referring to Figure 3.

Step 3. Fold the strip in half to make a loop; baste ends together to hold.

Completing the Stocking

Step 1. Place a pin at the center front and back of the cuff and stocking pieces.

Step 2. Slip the cuff inside the stocking with the front of the cuff facing you and the toe of the stocking facing to the left as shown in Figure 4; pin cuff at side seams and where center pins meet.

Figure 4

Step 3. Pin stocking loop between the stocking body and the front of the cuff at the right side seam with basted ends of loop up as shown in Figure 5; baste to hold. **Note:** *Be sure the loop sticks out so it is caught in the stitching.*

Figure 5

Step 4. Stitch layers together using a ⅜" seam allowance; trim seam to ¼" when finished.

Step 5. Turn cuff to the outside; press, if necessary. ❖

C

Add 9½" between lines at C and D to make complete stocking pattern

D

C   Add 9½" between lines at C and D
to make complete stocking pattern   B

Match on line to make complete pattern

Stocking
Cut 1 fusible fleece

A

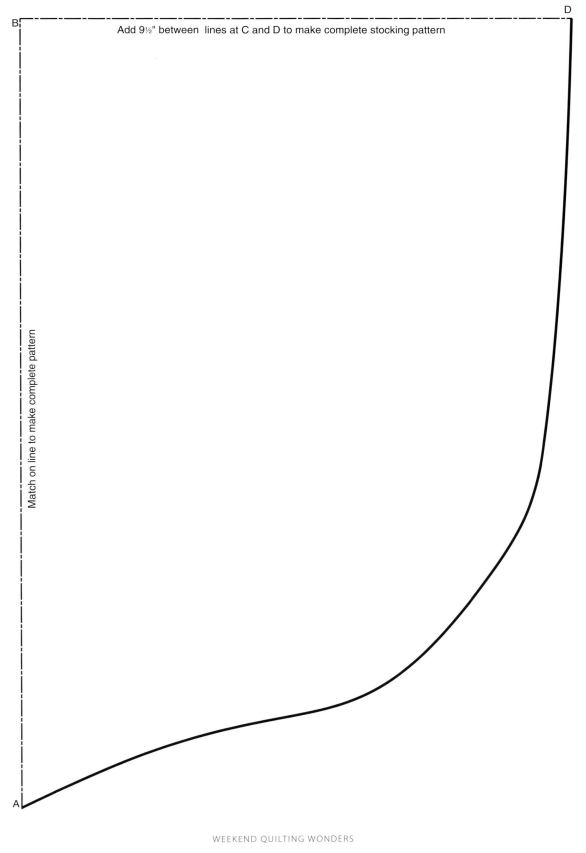

Add 9½" between lines at C and D to make complete stocking pattern

Match on line to make complete pattern

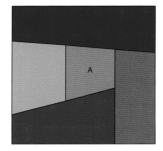

Christmas Rose
4" x 4" Block

Ready for Christmas

Dress up any outfit with a patchwork scarf and matching tote.

DESIGN BY CHRIS MALONE

Project Specifications
Skill Level: Intermediate
Tote Size: 14" x 12" x 3"
Scarf Size: 72½" x 5" (without leaves)
Key Ring Size: 4" x 4" (without clasp and ring)
Block Size: 4" x 4"
Number of Blocks: 23

Materials
- 8 fat quarters total assorted rose and cranberry prints
- 1 fat quarter gold metallic
- ⅝ yard cranberry print for tote lining
- ⅝ yard cranberry solid (home decorating–weight fabric)
- 1 yard dark green mottled
- Needled polyester batting: 6" x 76" strip for scarf and 12" x 12" square for leaves and key ring
- ¾ yard fusible fleece
- All-purpose thread to match fabrics
- Gold and dark green quilting or beading thread
- 8 or 9 dozen green rocailles glass beads
- 23 gold glass beads, size 6/0
- 2 (³⁄₁₆" diameter) dark green eyelets
- Brass findings for key ring: 1½"-long lobster clasp, 5"-

long ball chain and key ring
- 2⅞" x 13⅞" piece of cardboard or plastic needlework canvas for tote bottom
- 16 basting safety pins
- Eyelet pliers
- Basic sewing tools and supplies

Cutting
Step 1. Cut three 2" x 18" strips gold metallic. Subcut strips into 23 asymmetrical, four-sided A pieces for block centers. ***Note:*** *The sides of A in the sample range from 1¾"–2¼".*

Step 2. Cut three 2½" x 22" strips from each cranberry or rose fat quarter; subcut each strip into four 5" pieces to total 96.

Step 3. Cut two 6" x 38½" scarf backing strips dark green mottled.

Step 4. Cut four 2½" by fabric width binding strips dark green mottled.

Step 5. Cut five 1" by fabric width strips dark green mottled; subcut strips into (23) 4½" B, four 14½" C, two 3½" G and two 4½" H pieces.

Step 6. Cut one 4½" x 4½" backing square dark green mottled for key ring.

Step 7. Cut two 3½" x 14½" D strips, two 4½" x 14½" E strips, one 3½" x 39" F gusset strip and two 3" x 24" handle strips cranberry solid.

Step 8. Cut two 12½" x 14½" rectangles and one 3½" x 39" strip each cranberry print for lining and fusible fleece.

Step 9. Cut one 4½" x 4½" square batting from 12" batting square for key ring.

Completing the Christmas Rose Blocks

Step 1. Place one A piece right sides together in the center of one 2½" x 5" cranberry or rose print strip as shown in Figure 1; stitch.

Figure 1

Step 2. Flip A to the right side; press away from strip as shown in Figure 2; trim strip even with A, again referring to Figure 2.

Figure 2

Step 3. Place a second 2½" x 5" cranberry or rose print strip right sides together along the bottom edge of the stitched unit as shown in Figure 3; stitch as in Step 1.

Figure 3

Step 4. Trim seam allowance to ⅛"–¼" as shown in Figure 4; flip and press strip to the right side. Trim strip even with A, again referring to Figure 4.

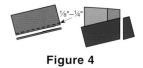

Figure 4

Step 5. Continue adding two more strips around the center as in Steps 1–4 to complete one block referring to the block drawing.

Step 6. Trim block to 4½" x 4½". ***Note:*** *The A piece does not have to be centered.*

Step 7. Repeat Steps 1–6 to complete 23 Christmas Rose blocks.

Making Leaf Shapes

Step 1. Prepare leaf template using pattern given on page 111. Trace six leaves on the wrong side of the dark green mottled.

Step 2. Fold fabric in half right sides together and pin to the remainder of the 12" batting square with traced side on top.

Step 3. Sew around each marked leaf shape, leaving an opening along one side as marked on pattern.

Step 4. Cut out ⅛" from seam; trim tip and turn right side out. Fold in seam allowance at opening; hand-stitch opening closed.

Completing the Scarf

Step 1. Join 16 blocks with 15 B strips to make one long strip referring to the Placement Diagram to complete the pieced top; press seams toward B strips.

Christmas Rose Skinny Scarf
Placement Diagram
72½" x 5" (without leaves)

Step 2. Join the two 6" x 38½" strips dark green mottled on the 6" ends to make one long strip; press seam open.

Step 3. Sandwich the 6" x 76" batting strip between the prepared backing piece and the pieced top; safety-pin layers together to hold.

Step 4. Machine-quilt in the ditch of seams on both sides of the B strips.

Step 5. When quilting is complete, remove safety pins; trim backing and batting even with the pieced top edges.

Step 6. Join binding strips on short ends to make one long strip; press seams open. Fold binding strip in half with wrong sides together along the length; press.

Step 7. Pin binding strip to the raw edges of the quilted scarf top; stitch all around, mitering corners and overlapping ends. Turn binding to the back side, leaving ½" showing on the front; hand-stitch to hold in place.

Step 8. To attach each leaf, prepare a needle with a doubled strand of dark green quilting or beading thread by pushing both ends of thread through the needle, leaving the loop at the end.

Step 9. Take a small stitch at the leaf center as marked on the pattern. Before pulling the thread through, insert the needle through the loop as shown in Figure 5. Pull thread taut, creating a knotless starting point.

Figure 5

Step 10. Slip 1" of beads (about 16 or 17) onto the needle and push down to the top of the leaf; take a small stitch into the center bottom edge of the scarf, letting the string of beads lay against the leaf center.

Step 11. Take a small stitch at the top of the leaf and again into the scarf; knot and clip thread. Repeat to add a leaf to each side of the center leaf and to add a matching set of three leaves on the other end of the scarf.

Step 12. Use gold quilting or beading thread to sew one gold bead to the center of each block.

Completing the Tote

Step 1. Join three Christmas Rose blocks with four B strips to make a block strip as shown in Figure 6; press seams toward B strips. Repeat to make two block strips.

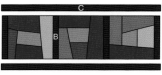

Figure 6

Step 2. Sew a C strip to opposite sides of each block strip, again referring to Figure 6; press seams toward C strips.

Step 3. Sew a D strip to one long side and an E strip to the opposite long side of one block strip to complete one side of the tote as shown in Figure 7; press seams toward D and E. Repeat to make the second side.

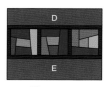

Figure 7

Christmas Rose Tote
Placement Diagram
14" x 12" x 3"

Step 4. Follow manufacturer's instructions to bond matching fusible fleece pieces to the wrong side of the pieced tote front and back pieces and to the F gusset strip, fusing from the center to the outside edges.

Step 5. Pin and stitch one long edge of the fused F strip down one side, across the E edge and up the remaining side of the tote front as shown in Figure 8. Trim the end of F even with ends of bag front.

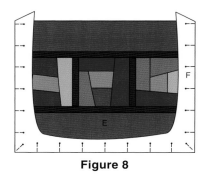

Figure 8

Step 6. Repeat Step 5 on the tote back to complete the tote shell. Press, clip seams and turn right side out.

Step 7. Fold each handle strip in half with right sides together along the length; stitch along the long edges to make tubes, leaving ends open.

Step 8. Turn tubes right side out and press, bringing seams to the center of each strip as shown in Figure 9.

Step 9. Topstitch along both long edges of each strip ¼" from the edges, again referring to Figure 9.

Figure 9

Step 10. Pin ends of one strip onto the right side of one top edge 2¾" from side seams, matching raw edges at the top as shown in Figure 10. Stitch in place; repeat on the opposite side of the tote to finish handles.

Figure 10

Step 11. Use gold quilting or beading thread to sew one gold bead to the center of each block in each block strip.

Step 12. Join lining pieces as in Steps 5 and 6 for tote. Fold under the upper raw edge of the lining ¼" and press.

Step 13. Fold tote handles up and press ¼" under all around the top of the tote.

Step 14. Place the needlepoint mesh or cardboard rectangle in the bottom of the tote; insert lining into the tote shell, matching side seams. Slipstitch the folded edge of the lining to the folded edge of the tote.

Step 15. Topstitch ¼" from the top edge of the tote to finish.

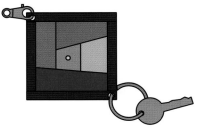

Christmas Rose Key Ring
Placement Diagram
4" x 4" (without clasp and ring)

Completing the Key Ring

Step 1. Trim the remaining Christmas Rose block to 3½" x 3½".

Step 2. Sew a G strip to opposite sides and H strips to the remaining sides of the block; press seams toward the G and H strips.

Step 3. Stack block and backing square right sides together on top of the same-size batting square; sew all around, leaving a 3" opening on one side. Trim batting close to seam and clip corners. Turn right side out through opening; press. Hand-stitch opening closed.

Step 4. Machine-quilt in the ditch of border seams.

Step 5. Use eyelet pliers to insert a green eyelet in two opposite corners of the quilted block.

Step 6. Insert key ring in one eyelet and lobster clasp in the second eyelet.

Step 7. Thread chain through ring on lobster clasp. Wrap chain around one handle of the tote bag and close. ❖

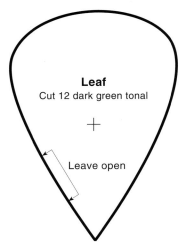

Leaf
Cut 12 dark green tonal

+

Leave open

Do You Hear What I Hear

Freezer-paper appliqué helps to make smooth edges on the

appliqué shapes on this quick-to-stitch holiday wall quilt.

DESIGN BY JOAN KARAGAVOORIAN

Project Specifications
Skill Level: Intermediate
Quilt Size: 20½" x 20½"

Materials
- Scraps gold, tan, orange, red, medium and dark greens, blue and brown
- 6" x 12" rectangle white tonal for snowman
- 5" x 16" rectangle white tonal for snow
- 15" x 15" A square blue print
- ⅛ yard burgundy tonal
- ¼ yard tan solid
- ⅓ yard cream print (¾ yard if directional as in sample)
- Backing 26" x 26"
- Batting 26" x 26"
- All-purpose thread to match fabrics
- Quilting thread
- Gold and silver pearl cotton No. 5
- Blue and black embroidery floss
- Black and brown permanent fabric pens
- Freezer paper
- 2 (⅜") and 5 (¼") black buttons
- 6 (4mm) black beads
- 1 black seed bead
- Washable marker or pencil
- Basic sewing tools and supplies

Cutting
Step 1. Cut two 1¼" x 15" B strips and two 1¼" x 16½" C strips burgundy tonal.

Step 2. Cut four 2¾" x 22" D strips cream print. **Note:** *If using a directional print as in the sample, cut two strips along the fabric length and then the remaining two strips along the remaining fabric width.*

Step 3. Cut three 2¼" by fabric width strips tan solid for binding.

Step 4. Trace each appliqué shape onto the dull side of freezer paper using patterns given; cut out shapes on drawn lines.

Step 5. Place the shiny side of the freezer-paper

shapes against the wrong side of fabrics as directed on patterns for color; iron in place. **Note:** *Sew dart in hat piece before ironing to freezer paper.*

Step 6. Cut out shapes, adding a ¼" seam allowance beyond the freezer-paper edges. Mark detail lines on each piece referring to patterns.

Completing the Quilt

Step 1. Clip inside curve seam allowance on each appliqué shape. Finger-press fabric seam allowances over the edges of the freezer paper to make finished shapes. **Note:** *Do not turn under edges of pieces that will lie under another piece.*

Step 2. Arrange the shapes on A in numerical order referring to the patterns and Placement Diagram for positioning. Hand-stitch pieces in place using all-purpose thread to match fabrics.

Step 3. Trace message and star trail onto A using a window or light box and a washable marker or pencil.

Step 4. Trace musical notes using the black permanent fabric pen and the lamb's-leg detail using the brown permanent fabric pen.

Step 5. Use a backstitch and 2 strands of blue embroidery floss to stitch the words; repeat with black to stitch arm lines on the snowman's jacket.

Step 6. Use a running stitch and 2 strands of blue embroidery floss for snowman's front and sleeve details.

Step 7. Use a backstitch and 2 strands of black embroidery floss for notes; add a French knot at the bottom of each note.

Step 8. Use a running stitch and gold pearl cotton to stitch star trail.

Step 9. Sew buttons and beads in place as marked on patterns.

Do You Hear What I Hear
Placement Diagram
20½" x 20½"

Step 10. Trim the appliquéd A square to 15" x 15".

Step 11. Sew B strips to the top and bottom and C strips to opposite sides of the appliquéd A square; press seams toward B and C strips.

Step 12. Center and sew a D strip to each side of the pieced center, mitering corners; press seams toward D strips.

Step 13. Trim seam to ¼"; press open to complete the top.

Step 14. Complete the quilt referring to Completing Your Quilt on page 170 using silver pearl cotton to quilt wind lines. ❖

16
blue scrap

red scrap   14

pleat

blue scrap

white tonal

15

orange scrap 13   12

7

11   10
red scrap   white tonal   red scrap

9   8
blue   blue
scrap   scrap

6
white tonal

Snowman Motif
Cut as directed

Do you hear what what I hear

Message

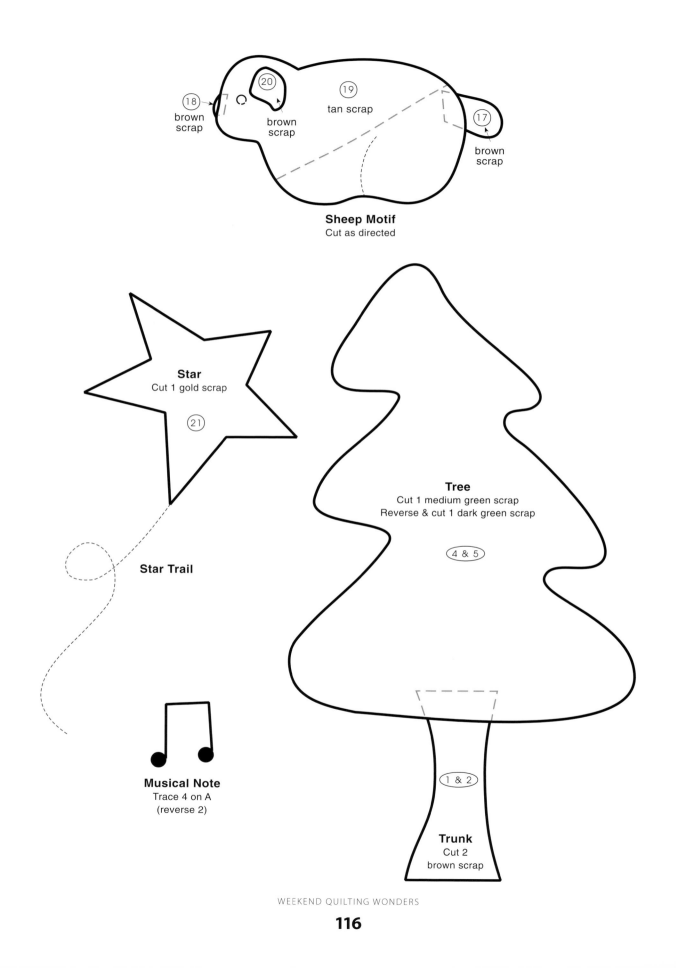

Sheep Motif
Cut as directed

(18) brown scrap
(20) brown scrap
(19) tan scrap
(17) brown scrap

Star
Cut 1 gold scrap
(21)

Star Trail

Tree
Cut 1 medium green scrap
Reverse & cut 1 dark green scrap
(4 & 5)

Musical Note
Trace 4 on A
(reverse 2)

(1 & 2)

Trunk
Cut 2
brown scrap

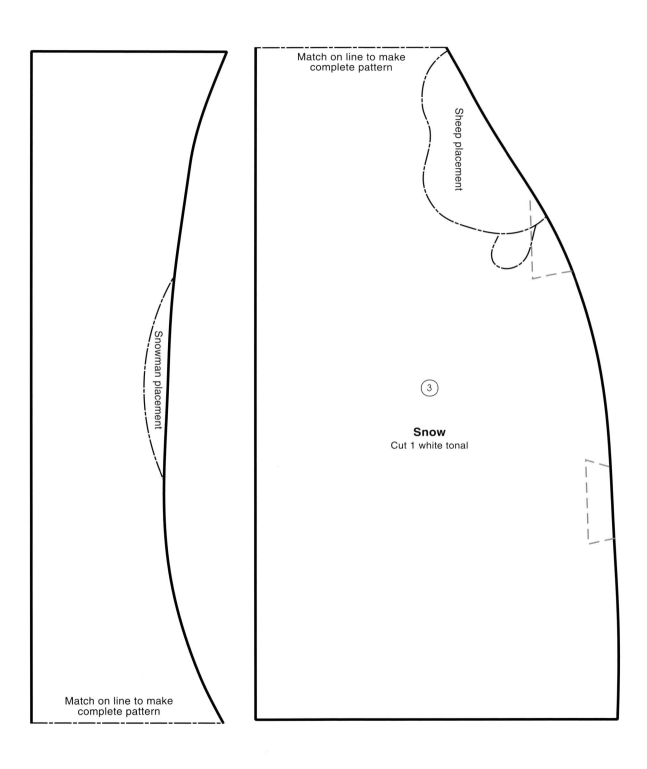

Match on line to make
complete pattern

Sheep placement

Snowman placement

③

Snow
Cut 1 white tonal

Match on line to make
complete pattern

Rudolph
6" x 9¼" Block

Rudolph Gift Bag

Give a gift of love inside this pretty holiday gift bag.

DESIGN BY CHRISTINE SCHULTZ

Project Specifications
Skill Level: Beginner
Bag Size: 14" x 20¼" x 2½"
Block Size: 6" x 9¼"
Number of Blocks: 1

Materials
All fabrics are flannel
- 3½" x 6" rectangle multicolor print
- 1½" x 1½" square red solid
- ⅛ yard each cream print and medium brown mottled
- ⅛ yard dark brown tonal
- ½ yard lining fabric
- ¾ yard red print
- All-purpose thread to match fabrics
- Brown embroidery floss
- 2 (⅜") black ball buttons
- 2 yards ribbon or rattail cord
- White nail polish
- Beads (optional)
- Basic sewing tools and supplies

Cutting
Step 1. Prepare copies of paper-piecing patterns as directed.
Step 2. Cut one copy of each pattern along solid lines. Use the paper pieces as templates to cut fabric pieces as directed on patterns for color, adding at least ¼" all around when cutting for seam allowance.
Step 3. Prepare the ear template using pattern given; cut as directed on the pattern, adding a ¼" seam allowance all around.
Step 4. Cut two 4½" x 9¾" A strips red print.
Step 5. Cut one 4½" x 14½" B strip and one 7½" x 14½" C strip red print.
Step 6. Cut a 14½" x 20¾" rectangle red print for the bag back.
Step 7. Cut two 4½" x 14½" strips red print for lining top.
Step 8. Cut two 16¾" x 14½" lining pieces.

Completing the Paper-Pieced Units
Step 1. Set your machine to a small stitch length to make paper removal easier later.

Figure 4   **Figure 5**

Step 5. Trim the 1-2 seam allowance to ⅛"–¼" as shown in Figure 5. Fold fabric 2 to cover area 2; lightly press with a warm dry iron.

Step 6. Continue to add fabric pieces in numerical order to cover the paper pattern as shown in Figure 6.

Figure 6   **Figure 7**

Step 7. Pin outside fabric edges to paper pattern. Trim paper and fabric edges even on the outside heavy solid line as shown in Figure 7 to complete one paper-pieced unit.

Step 8. Place two ear pieces right sides together; stitch around curved edge. Trim seam and point, turn right side out and press. Repeat to make two ears.

Step 9. Pleat ear pieces on the dotted line as indicated on pattern; baste to hold.

Step 10. Insert the stitched ear pieces between seams as indicated on paper pattern and as shown in Figure 8.

Figure 8

Step 2. Select one paper-piecing section. Place fabric to cover area 1 on paper pattern with wrong side of fabric against the unmarked side of the paper, allowing fabric to extend at least ¼" into adjacent areas as shown in Figure 1.

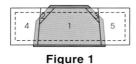

Figure 1

Step 3. Place fabric for area 2 right sides together with fabric 1 on the 1-2 edge as shown in Figure 2; pin along the 1-2 line. Fold fabric 2 over to cover area 2, allowing fabric to extend at least ¼" into adjacent areas as shown in Figure 3. Adjust fabric if necessary. Unfold fabric 2 to lie flat on fabric 1; pin in place. **Note:** *Check that each piece will cover its area before stitching.*

Step 11. Repeat Steps 2–7 to complete all paper-pieced units.

Completing the Bag Front

Step 1. Arrange paper-pieced units as shown in Figure 9; press seams in the direction of the arrows, again referring to Figure 9.

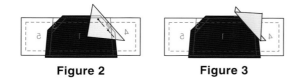

Figure 2   **Figure 3**

Step 4. Flip paper pattern; stitch on the 1-2 line beginning and ending 2 or 3 stitches into adjacent areas as shown in Figure 4. **Note:** *On edge pieces, stitch to the outside edge of the pattern.*

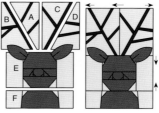

Figure 9

Step 2. Fold the 3½" x 6" multicolor rectangle in half with right sides together along the length; stitch around three sides, leaving a small opening for turning on the long side as shown in Figure 10; turn right side out through opening and press.

Figure 10

Step 3. Tie a knot in the stitched strip to make a bow tie; hand-stitch the bow tie to Rudolph's neck area.

Step 4. Stem-stitch the mouth shape using 2 strands brown embroidery floss referring to pattern for positioning.

Step 5. Place a dot of white nail polish on each ⅜" black ball button; let dry.

Step 6. When dry, sew buttons to the head area referring to pattern for placement to complete the block.

Step 7. Sew an A strip to opposite long sides of the pieced block; press seams toward A strips.

Step 8. Sew B to the bottom and C to the top of the pieced block to complete the bag front; press seams toward B and C strips.

Step 9. Remove paper foundations.

Completing the Bag

Step 1. Lay the bag front and back pieces right sides together; pin. Sew around sides and bottom, leaving the top edge open; press seams open.

Step 2. Fold one bottom corner of the bag so the side and bottom seams are aligned as shown in Figure 11.

Figure 11   **Figure 12**

Step 3. Mark a sewing line perpendicular to the seam and 1¼" from the bottom corner as shown in Figure 12; stitch on the marked line. Trim seam to ¼"; repeat on the opposite corner.

Step 4. Sew a 4½" x 14½" strip red print to the top of each lining piece; press seam toward lining pieces.

Step 5. Join the lining pieces right sides together and stitch corners referring to Steps 1–4 except leave a 4" opening along the bottom edge.

Rudolph Gift Bag
Placement Diagram
14" x 20¼" x 2½"

Step 6. With the outer bag right side out and lining wrong side out, slide the outer bag inside of the lining. Align and stitch around the top raw edge.

Step 7. Turn the entire piece right side out through the opening in the lining seam; hand- or machine-stitch the opening closed. Push the lining inside the bag; press the top edge.

Step 8. To make the drawstring channel, sew a line of stitches around the top of the bag 3" from the top edge, overlapping stitches at the beginning and end. Sew a second line of stitches ½" below this stitched line.

Step 9. Use a seam ripper to cut one thread in each side seam between the channel stitching lines as shown in Figure 13.

Figure 13

Step 10. Cut two 34"-long pieces rattail cord or ribbon; feed each through the side-seam openings in opposite directions and knot ends together. Add beads to the ends, if desired. ❖

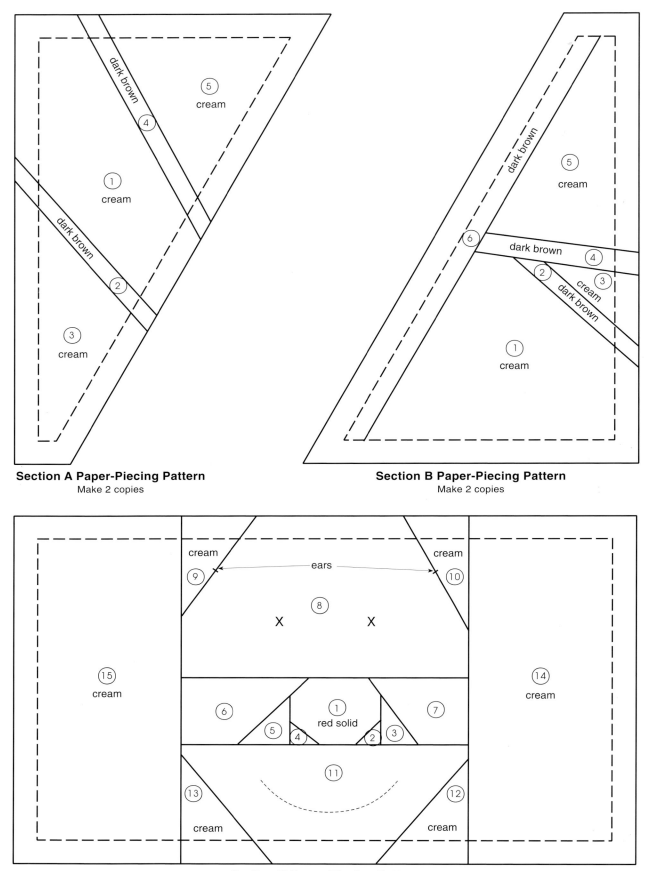

Section A Paper-Piecing Pattern
Make 2 copies

Section B Paper-Piecing Pattern
Make 2 copies

Section E Paper-Piecing Pattern
Make 2 copies
Use medium brown mottled in all unmarked areas.

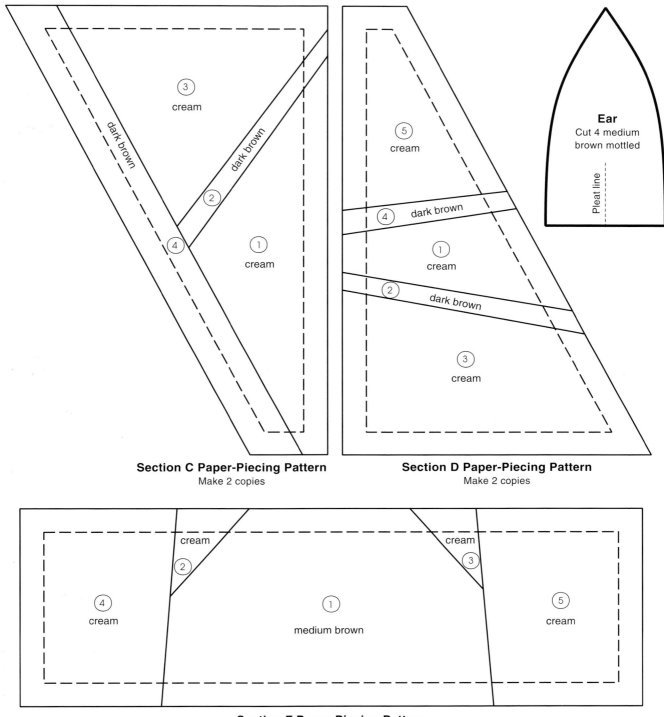

Section C Paper-Piecing Pattern
Make 2 copies

Section D Paper-Piecing Pattern
Make 2 copies

Ear
Cut 4 medium
brown mottled

Pleat line

Section F Paper-Piecing Pattern
Make 2 copies

Tree Time Table Setting

Trees reach for the stars in this table topper and coaster set.

DESIGNS BY JILL REBER

Project Specifications
Skill Level: Beginner
Quilt Size: 22⅝" x 22⅝"
Coaster Size: 4" x 4"

Materials
- Scraps brown and 4 different dark green tonals
- ⅛ yard gold print
- ⅓ yard cream tonal
- ½ yard holly print
- ⅔ yard red tonal
- Backing 28" x 28"
- Batting 28" x 28" and (4) 4½" x 4" squares
- All-purpose thread to match fabrics
- Quilting thread
- ⅛ yard 18"-wide fusible web
- Basic sewing tools and supplies

Cutting
Step 1. Cut one 4½" by fabric width strip red tonal; subcut strip into nine 4½" A squares.

Step 2. Cut three 2½" by fabric width strips red tonal; subcut strips into four each 11" F and 13" G rectangles.

Step 3. Cut three 2¼" by fabric width strips red tonal for binding.

Step 4. Cut four 2½" x 4½" B rectangles each dark green tonal.

Step 5. Cut two 2½" by fabric width strips cream tonal; subcut strips into (32) 2½" C squares. Draw a diagonal line from corner to corner on the wrong side of each square.

Step 6. Cut one 2" by fabric width strip cream tonal; subcut strip into eight 4½" D rectangles.

Step 7. Cut four 1½" x 4½" E pieces brown tonal.

Step 8. Cut one 12½" x 12½" square holly print; cut the square on both diagonals to make four H triangles.

Step 9. Trace five star shapes onto the paper side of the fusible web; fuse to the wrong side of the gold print.

Step 10. Cut out star shapes on traced lines; remove paper backing.

Completing the Table Topper

Step 1. Referring to Figure 1, place a C square on one end of B; stitch on the marked line. Trim seam to ¼" and press C to the right side.

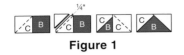
Figure 1

Step 2. Repeat Step 1 with a C square on the opposite end of B to complete one B-C unit, again referring to Figure 1; repeat to make 16 B-C units.

Step 3. Select four different B-C units; join as shown in Figure 2 to complete a top unit; press seams in one direction. Repeat to make four top units.

Figure 2

Step 4. Sew E between two D pieces to make a trunk unit as shown in Figure 3; press seams toward E. Repeat to make four trunk units.

Figure 3

Step 5. Sew a trunk unit to a top unit to complete a tree unit as shown in Figure 4; press seams toward the trunk unit. Repeat to make four tree units.

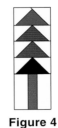
Figure 4

Step 6. Sew F to one short side and G to the opposite short side of H as shown in Figure 5; press seams toward F and G strips. Trim the ends of F and G even with the edge of H, again referring to Figure 5. Repeat to make four F-G-H units.

Figure 5

Step 7. Sew an F-G-H unit to opposite sides of two tree units to complete the side units as shown in Figure 6; press seams toward the F-G-H units.

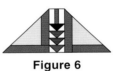
Figure 6

Step 8. Center and fuse a star shape to five A squares. Set aside four fused A squares for coasters.

Step 9. Sew a tree unit to opposite sides of the fused A square to complete the center row as shown in Figure 7; press seams toward the fused A square.

Figure 7

Step 10. Sew a side unit to opposite sides of the center row to complete the pieced top referring to Figure 8; press seams away from the center row.

Figure 8

Step 11. Complete the table topper referring to Completing Your Quilt on page 170.

Step 12. Using thread to match star shape, machine-zigzag around the star shape to finish.

Completing the Coasters

Step 1. Place a 4½" x 4½" batting square on a flat surface; place an unfused A square right side up on the batting square. Place a fused A square right sides together with the unfused A square; stitch all around, leaving 2" on one side unstitched.

Step 2. Trim batting close to seam; turn right side out through the opening.

Step 3. Turn the seam of the opening to the inside and hand-stitch closed; press.

Step 4. Using thread to match star shape, machine-zigzag around the star shape to finish. Repeat to make four coasters. ❖

Tree Time Table Topper
Placement Diagram
22⅝" x 22⅝"

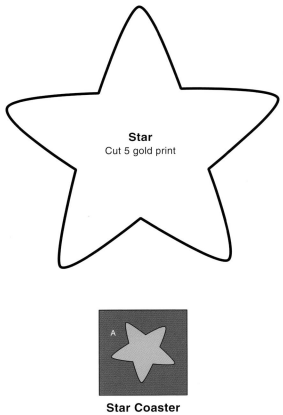

Star
Cut 5 gold print

Star Coaster
Placement Diagram
4" x 4"

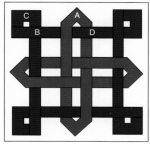

Celtic Christmas
7" x 7" Block

Celtic Christmas Table Runner

Interwoven pieces create the Celtic design in the blocks of this holiday runner.

DESIGN BY BARBARA CLAYTON

Project Specifications
Skill Level: Intermediate
Runner Size: 34½" x 14½"
Block Size: 7" x 7"
Number of Blocks: 3

Materials
- ⅛ yard red solid
- ⅛ yard dark green tonal 1
- ¼ yard Kelly green mottled
- ⅓ yard dark green tonal 2
- ⅜ yard red mottled
- ½ yard cream tonal
- Backing 39" x 19"
- Batting 39" x 19"
- All-purpose thread to match fabrics
- Quilting thread
- Clear nylon monofilament
- ⅛ yard fusible web
- Freezer paper
- Water-erasable marker or pencil
- Water-soluble glue sticks
- Basic sewing tools and supplies

Cutting
Step 1. Cut three 7½" x 7½" E squares cream tonal.
Step 2. Cut three 2¼" by fabric width strips cream tonal for binding.
Step 3. Cut one 11¼" x 11¼" square red mottled; cut the square on both diagonals to make four F triangles.
Step 4. Cut two 5⅞" x 5⅞" squares red mottled; cut each square in half on one diagonal to make four G triangles.
Step 5. Cut two 1¼" x 30½" H strips and two 1¼" x 12" I strips dark green tonal 2.
Step 6. Cut two 2" x 32" J strips and two 2" x 15" K strips Kelly green mottled.

Preparing the Appliqué Pieces
Step 1. Trace A–D patterns onto freezer paper as indicated on each piece.
Step 2. Press the waxy side of the freezer paper onto the wrong side of fabrics as directed on patterns for color and number to cut.
Step 3. Cut out fabric shapes, leaving ¼" beyond the edges of the freezer paper all around.
Step 4. Clip corners and indentations almost to the paper pattern.

Step 10. Fuse shapes to the wrong side of the dark green tonal 1; cut out shapes on marked lines. Remove paper backing.

Completing the Blocks

Step 1. Fold each E square and crease to mark the vertical, horizontal and diagonal centers.

Step 2. Transfer the full-size block drawing given to each E square using a water-erasable marker or pencil.

Step 3. Arrange, pin and baste pieces to each E square in numerical order as marked on the full-size pattern, tucking ends under other pieces as marked on pattern.

Step 4. Using clear nylon monofilament and a narrow machine blind-hem stitch, stitch all around the edges of each piece.

Step 5. Wet the back side of each block, cut a slit behind each appliqué piece and remove the freezer paper. Let dry; lightly press each block.

Completing the Quilt

Step 1. Join the blocks with the F and G triangles in diagonal rows as shown in Figure 2; press seams toward F and G.

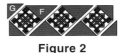

Figure 2

Step 2. Join the diagonal rows to complete the pieced center; press seams in one direction.

Step 3. Arrange and fuse holly leaves on the F and G triangles referring to the Placement Diagram for positioning.

Step 4. Sew H strips to opposite long sides and I strips to the short ends of the pieced center; press seams toward H and I strips.

Step 5. Sew J strips to opposite long sides and K strips to the short ends of the pieced center; press seams toward J and K strips to complete the pieced top.

Step 6. Arrange and pin yo-yo berries in place on holly leaves referring to the Placement Diagram.

Step 7. Prepare for quilting and complete referring to Completing Your Quilt on page 170, using thread to match fabrics and a machine blind-hem stitch to stitch around holly leaves and yo-yo berries during the quilting process. ❖

Step 5. Glue seam allowance to the freezer paper all the way around the edges of the A pieces; cut through the glued A pieces where indicated on pattern to allow for tucking under other pattern pieces.

Step 6. Glue edges under all around on remaining pieces, leaving ¼" unglued where indicated by dashed lines on each piece.

Step 7. Prepare template for the yo-yo circle; cut as directed.

Step 8. Turn one yo-yo circle edge under ⅛"; using a double thread and a running stitch, sew around folded edge referring to Figure 1. Pull the thread to gather the fabric tightly and knot off. Flatten the gathered circle to form a yo-yo berry. Repeat to make 16 yo-yo berries.

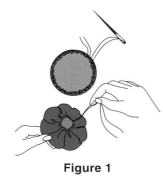

Figure 1

Step 9. Trace the holly leaf pattern onto the paper side of the fusible web as directed on pattern for number to cut; cut out shapes, leaving a margin around each one.

Yo-Yo Circle
Cut 16 red solid

Holly Leaf
Cut 12 dark
green tonal 1

Celtic Christmas Runner
Placement Diagram
34½" x 14½"

C
Cut 12 each dark green
tonal 2 & freezer paper

B
Cut 12 each dark green
tonal 2 & freezer paper

D
Cut 12 each dark green
tonal 2 & freezer paper

A
Cut 6 each red mottled & freezer paper

Cut here

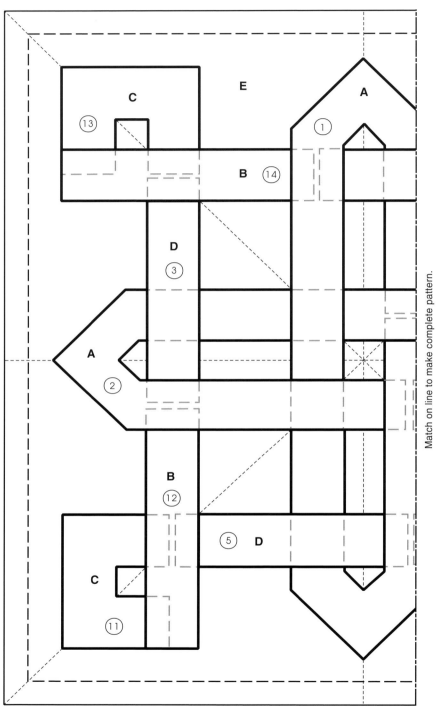

Match on line to make complete pattern.

Full-Size Block Drawing
Arrange pieces, tucking ends under as marked.

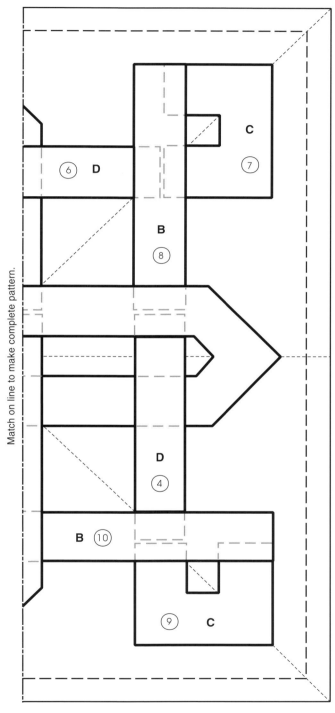

Match on line to make complete pattern.

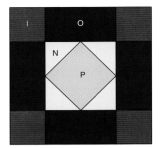

Center
8" x 8" Block
Make 1

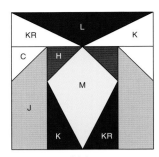

Side
8" x 8" Block
Make 4

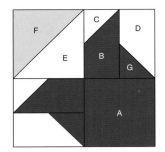

Tulip
8" x 8" Block
Make 4

Tulip Carousel Topper

Pieced tulips fill the corners of this colorful topper.

DESIGN BY BEA YURKERWICH

Project Specifications
Skill Level: Intermediate
Quilt Size: 30" x 30"
Block Size: 8" x 8"
Number of Blocks: 9

Materials
- ⅛ yard dark green print
- ¼ yard yellow mottled
- ¼ yard each light green print and light blue tonal
- ⅓ yard red print
- ⅜ yard medium blue solid
- ½ yard each dark blue print and dark blue mottled
- ½ yard white tonal
- Backing 36" x 36"
- Batting 36" x 36"
- All-purpose thread to match fabrics
- Quilting thread
- Basic sewing tools and supplies

Cutting
Step 1. Cut one 4½" by fabric width strip red print; subcut strip into four 4½" A squares and eight 2½" B rectangles.

Step 2. Cut one 2½" by fabric width strip red print; subcut strip into eight 2½" G squares.

Step 3. Cut two 2½" by fabric width strips white tonal; subcut strips into (16) 2½" C squares and eight 4½" D rectangles.

Step 4. Cut two 4⅞" x 4⅞" squares each white (E) and light blue tonals (F); cut each square in half on one diagonal to make four each E and F triangles.

Step 5. Cut one 4½" x 4½" P square light blue tonal.

Step 6. Cut four 2⅞" x 2⅞" squares dark green print; cut each square in half on one diagonal to make eight I triangles.

Step 7. Cut four 2½" x 2½" H squares dark green print.

Step 8. Cut two 2½" by fabric width strips light green print; subcut strips into eight 6½" J strips.

Step 9. Cut four 2½" x 4½" O rectangles dark blue print.

Step 10. Cut four 2½" x 2½" N squares yellow mottled.

Step 11. Cut two 3½" x 24½" Q strips and two 3½" x 30½" R strips dark blue mottled.

Step 12. Cut four 2¼" by fabric width strips medium blue solid for binding.

Step 13. Prepare templates using patterns given; cut as directed on each piece.

Completing the Tulip Blocks

Step 1. Draw a diagonal line from corner to corner on the wrong side of the C and G squares; set aside eight C squares for the Side blocks.

Step 2. Referring to Figure 1, place C right sides together on one end of B; stitch on the marked line. Trim seam to ¼" and press C to the right side to complete one B-C unit; repeat to make four B-C units and four reversed B-C units, again referring to Figure 1.

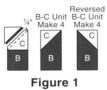

Figure 1

Step 3. Repeat Step 2 to make four D-G and four reversed D-G units as shown in Figure 2.

Figure 2

Step 4. Sew E to F along the diagonal; repeat to make four E-F units.

Step 5. To complete one Tulip block, sew a B-C unit to a D-G unit to make a B-C-D-G unit as shown in Figure 3; press seams toward the B-C unit. Repeat to make a reversed unit, again referring to Figure 3.

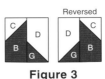

Figure 3

Step 6. Sew a B-C-D-G unit to an E-F unit as shown in Figure 4; press seams toward the E-F unit.

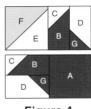

Figure 4

Step 7. Sew a reversed B-C-D-G unit to A, again referring to Figure 4; press seam toward A.

Step 8. Join the pieced units to complete one Tulip block referring to the block drawing; press seams in one direction. Repeat to make four Tulip blocks.

Completing the Side Blocks

Step 1. Referring to Figure 5 and Step 1 for Completing the Tulip Blocks, complete four C-J and four reversed C-J units.

Figure 5

Step 2. Sew H and dark blue print K and KR pieces to M to complete an H-K-M unit as shown in Figure 6; press seams away from M. Repeat to make four units.

Figure 6

Step 3. Sew a white tonal K and KR to L to complete a K-L unit as shown in Figure 7; press seams toward L. Repeat to make four K-L units.

Figure 7

Step 4. To complete one Side block, sew a C-J and reversed C-J unit to opposite sides of an H-K-M unit as shown in Figure 8; press seams toward the C-J units.

Figure 8

Step 5. Sew a K-L unit to the H end of the previously pieced unit referring to the block drawing to complete one Side block; press seam toward the K-L unit. Repeat to make four Side blocks.

Completing the Center Block
Step 1. Mark a diagonal line from corner to corner on the wrong side of each N square.
Step 2. Referring to Figure 9, sew N right sides together on opposite corners of P; trim seam allowance to ¼" and press N to the right side. Repeat on the remaining corners of P to complete the N-P unit, again referring to Figure 9.

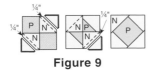

Figure 9

Step 3. Sew O to opposite sides of the N-P unit to make the center row; press seams toward O.
Step 4. Sew I to opposite ends of O; press seams toward O. Repeat to make two I-O units.

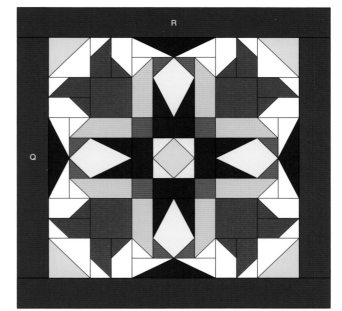

Tulip Carousel Topper
Placement Diagram
30" x 30"

Step 5. Sew an I-O unit to opposite sides of the center row to complete one Center block; press seams toward the I-O units.

Completing the Quilt
Step 1. Sew a Side block between two Tulip blocks to make a row referring to the Placement Diagram for positioning of blocks; press seams toward the Tulip blocks. Repeat to make two Tulip rows.
Step 2. Sew a Side block to opposite sides of the Center block, again referring to the Placement Diagram for positioning; press seams toward the Center block.
Step 3. Sew the Center row between the two Tulip rows to complete the pieced center; press seams toward the Center row.
Step 4. Sew a Q strip to opposite sides and R strips to the remaining sides to complete the top; press seams toward Q and R strips.
Step 5. Complete the quilt referring to Completing Your Quilt on page 170. ❖

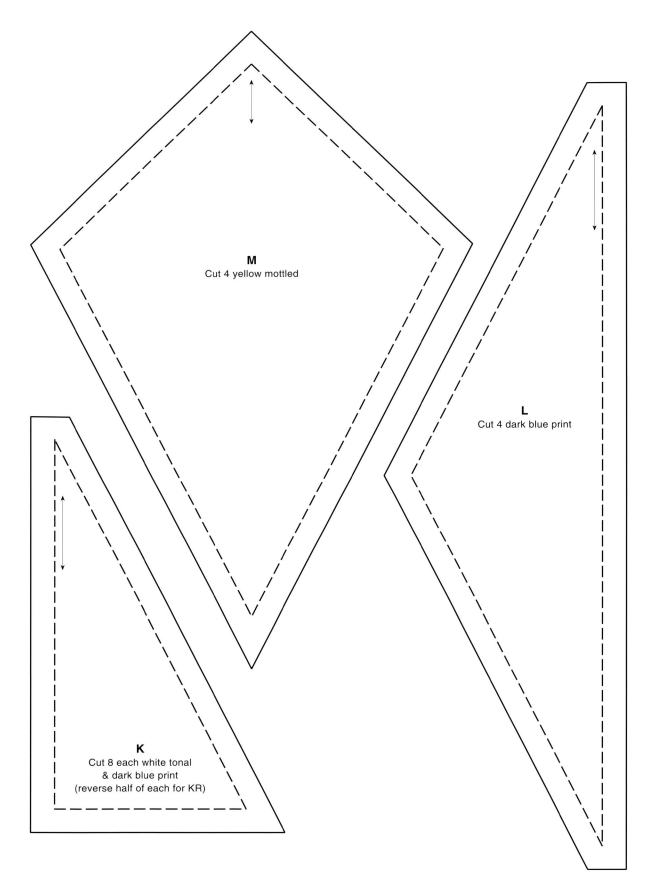

M
Cut 4 yellow mottled

L
Cut 4 dark blue print

K
Cut 8 each white tonal
& dark blue print
(reverse half of each for KR)

Pleasingly Paisley Table Topper

Stitch up this simple table topper with a colorful paisley print.

Use it on your table to highlight your favorite centerpiece.

DESIGN BY TOBY LISCHKO

Project Specifications
Skill Level: Beginner
Topper Size: 38" x 38"

Materials
- ⅜ yard gold tonal
- ⅝ yard green tonal
- ⅝ yard cream tonal
- 1 yard wine paisley
- Backing 44" x 44"
- Batting 44" x 44"
- All-purpose thread to match fabrics
- Quilting thread
- Basic sewing tools and supplies

Cutting
Step 1. Cut two 6⅞" by fabric width strips cream tonal; subcut strips into eight 6⅞" squares. Cut each square in half on one diagonal to make 16 A triangles.

Step 2. Cut one 2⅞" by fabric width strip each cream (D) and gold (F) tonals; subcut D strip into (12) 2⅞" squares and F strip into (14) 2⅞" squares. Cut each square in half on one diagonal to make 24 D and 28 F triangles.

Step 3. Cut one 6⅞" by fabric width strip each green (B) and gold (C) tonals; subcut B strip into six 6⅞" squares and C strip into two 6⅞" squares. Cut each square in half on one diagonal to make 12 B and four C triangles.

Step 4. Cut two 2⅞" by fabric width strips green tonal; subcut strips into (26) 2⅞" squares. Cut each square in half on one diagonal to make 52 E triangles.

Step 5. Cut one 5⅞" by fabric width strip each wine paisley (H) and green tonal (I); subcut each strip into two 5⅞" squares. Cut each square in half on one diagonal to make four each H and I triangles.

Step 6. Cut four 5½" x 28½" G strips wine paisley.

Completing the Quilt

Step 1. Sew B to A along the diagonal to make an A-B unit as shown in Figure 1; press seam toward B. Repeat to make 12 A-B units.

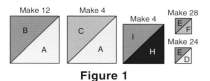

Figure 1

Step 2. Repeat Step 1 with A and C, H and I, D and E, and E and F to make four each A-C and H-I units, 24 D-E units and 28 E-F units, again referring to Figure 1.

Step 3. Arrange the A-B and A-C units and join to make rows referring to Figure 2; press seams in adjacent rows in opposite directions. Join the rows to complete the pieced center; press seams in one direction.

Figure 2

Step 4. Join six each E-F and D-E units to make a side strip as shown in Figure 3; press seams away from the center of the strip. Repeat to make two side strips.

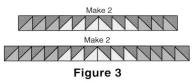

Figure 3

Step 5. Sew a side strip to opposite sides of the pieced center; press seams away from the side strips.

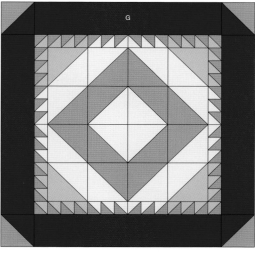

Pleasingly Paisley Table Topper
Placement Diagram
38" x 38"

Step 6. Join six D-E units and eight E-F units to make the top strip, again referring to Figure 3; press seams away from the center of the strip. Repeat to make the bottom strip.

Step 7. Sew the pieced strips to the top and bottom of the pieced center; press seams away from the strips.

Step 8. Sew a G strip to opposite sides of the pieced center; press seams toward the G strips.

Step 9. Sew an H-I unit to each end of the remaining G strips as shown in Figure 4; press seams toward the G strips.

Figure 4

Step 10. Sew the G-H-I strips to the top and bottom of the pieced center; press seams toward the G-H-I strips

Figure 5

Step 11. Complete the quilt referring to Completing Your Quilt on page 170, except trim the batting even with the quilted top and trim the backing ¾" larger all around. Turn under the edge of the backing ¼"; press. Bring the folded backing to the front side, covering outer edge, and machine-stitch in place as shown in Figure 5 to finish. ❖

It Hits the Spot Runner

Black and white is accented with red in this contemporary runner and
napkin-ring set. Ribbon and yo-yos create the rings.

DESIGNS BY CHRIS MALONE

Project Specifications
Skill Level: Beginner
Runner Size: Approximately 48" x 12"

Materials
- Scrap white-with-black dot for napkin holders
- ⅛ yard each 7 black-with-white prints
- ⅛ yard each 3 white-with-black prints
- ⅔ yard red mottled
- ⅝ yard black-with-white print for napkins
- Backing 54" x 18"
- Batting 54" x 18"
- All-purpose thread to match fabrics
- Quilting thread
- 48" red 1½"-wide wire-edged ribbon
- ¼ yard lightweight fusible interfacing
- Scrap Timtex interfacing or cardboard for napkin holders
- 2 red/black ⅞" buttons
- Seam sealant
- Basic sewing tools and supplies

Cutting
Step 1. Cut black-with-white prints into approximately 22 assorted strips 12½" long and 2"–3" wide.
Step 2. Prepare templates using patterns given; cut as directed on each piece, cutting interfacing to the size of the pattern and adding a ¼" seam allowance to fabric pieces when cutting.
Step 3. Cut four 2¼" by fabric width strips red mottled for binding.
Step 4. Cut two 16" x 16" squares each black-with-white print and red mottled for napkins.

Completing the Runner
Step 1. Arrange black print strips side by side, mixing widths and prints. When satisfied with arrangement, join strips to make the runner base.

Step 2. Center and bond a fusible interfacing circle to the wrong side of a corresponding-size fabric circle; repeat with all circles.

Step 3. Arrange the circles on the runner base, varying sizes and prints. When satisfied with arrangement, turn edges of circles under to the edge of the interfacing; hand or machine-stitch in place.

Step 4. Complete the runner referring to Completing Your Quilt on page 170.

Completing the Napkins & Napkin Holders

Step 1. Pin one 16" x 16" black-with-white print square right sides together with a red mottled square; sew all around, leaving a 3" opening along one edge. Trim corners and turn right side out; press. Repeat with second set of squares.

Step 2. Fold in seam allowance of the openings; press and slipstitch closed.

Step 3. Topstitch ¼" from edges using black thread.

Step 4. Apply seam sealant to the edges of each yo-yo circle.

Step 5. Referring to Figure 1 and using a doubled thread, hand-sew a line of gathering stitches ⅛" from the edge of each circle. Place a yo-yo interfacing circle on the wrong side of the fabric and pull the stitches to gather tightly together in the center.

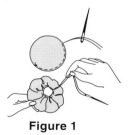

Figure 1

Step 6. Cut the ribbon into two 24" lengths; cut a V shape in each end of each piece.

Step 7. Place one yo-yo on one ribbon length about 10" from one end and sew a button on the center of the yo-yo through the ribbon. Repeat with second yo-yo and ribbon length.

Step 8. Fold the napkin as desired and wrap ribbon around back and tie in a loose knot at the side to finish. ❖

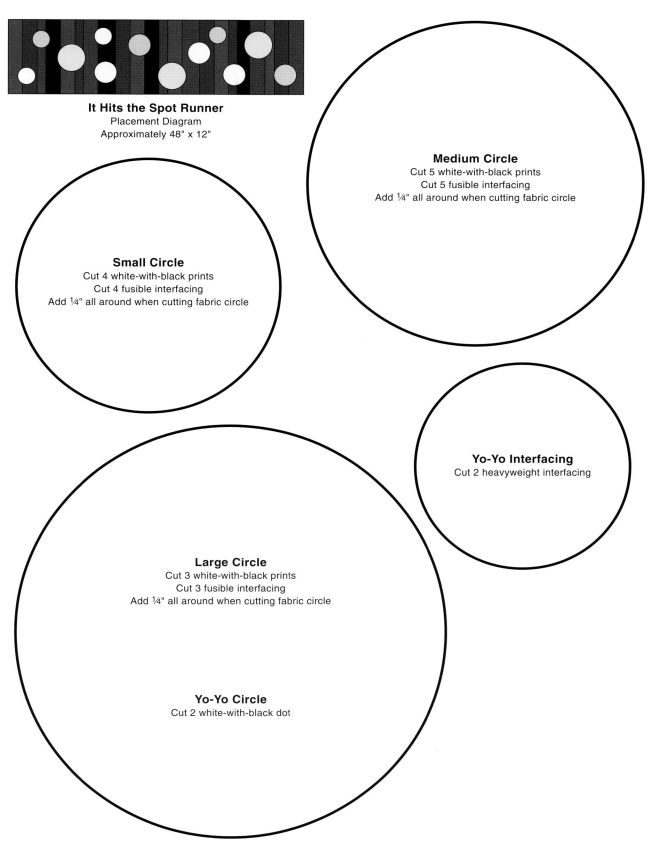

It Hits the Spot Runner
Placement Diagram
Approximately 48" x 12"

Small Circle
Cut 4 white-with-black prints
Cut 4 fusible interfacing
Add ¼" all around when cutting fabric circle

Medium Circle
Cut 5 white-with-black prints
Cut 5 fusible interfacing
Add ¼" all around when cutting fabric circle

Yo-Yo Interfacing
Cut 2 heavyweight interfacing

Large Circle
Cut 3 white-with-black prints
Cut 3 fusible interfacing
Add ¼" all around when cutting fabric circle

Yo-Yo Circle
Cut 2 white-with-black dot

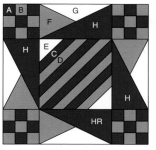

Easy Blue
18" x 18" Block
Make 2

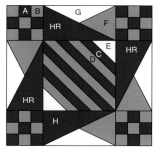

Easy Blue Reversed
18" x 18" Block
Make 2

Easy Blue Table Topper

This easy topper uses shades of blue. Choose your own color scheme to match your decor or use reds and greens for a Christmas quilt.

DESIGN BY CONNIE RAND

Project Specifications
Skill Level: Intermediate
Topper Size: 36" x 36"
Block Size: 18" x 18"
Number of Blocks: 4

Materials
- ⅜ yard navy/gold print
- ⅞ yard white tonal
- ⅞ yard blue print
- 1⅓ yards navy mottled
- Backing 42" x 42"
- Batting 42" x 42"
- All-purpose thread to match fabrics
- Quilting thread
- Template material
- Basic sewing tools and supplies

Cutting
Step 1. Cut five 2" by fabric width strips each navy mottled (A) and blue print (B); subcut two strips each fabric in half to make four half-strips each. Discard one half-strip each fabric.

Step 2. Cut four 1½" by fabric width strips each navy mottled (C) and blue print (D).

Step 3. Cut four 2¼" by fabric width strips navy/gold print for binding.

Step 4. Cut one 4¼" by fabric width strip white tonal; subcut strip into four 4¼" squares. Cut each square in half on one diagonal to make eight E triangles.

Step 5. Prepare templates for F, G and H using patterns given; cut as directed.

Piecing the Units
Step 1. Sew a B strip between two A strips to make an A-B-A strip set; press seams toward A. Repeat to make one A-B-A half-strip.

Step 2. Cut the strip sets into (24) 2" A-B-A units as shown in Figure 1.

Step 3. Sew an A strip between two B strips to make a B-A-B strip set; press seams toward A. Repeat to make one B-A-B half-strip.

Step 4. Cut the strip sets into (24) 2" B-A-B units, again referring to Figure 1.

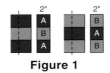

Figure 1

Step 5. Sew a B-A-B unit between two A-B-A units to make an A corner unit as shown in Figure 2; press seams in one direction. Repeat to make eight A corner units.

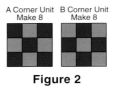

Figure 2

Step 6. Sew an A-B-A unit between two B-A-B units to make a B corner unit, again referring to Figure 2; press seams in one direction. Repeat to make eight B corner units.

Step 7. Join two each C and D strips to make a strip set, alternating fabrics; press seams toward C strips. Repeat to make two strip sets.

Step 8. Prepare a template for C-D using the pattern given. Place the template on the strip sets to cut four

C-D and four D-C pieces, aligning lines on template with seams of the strip set and rotating template top to bottom as shown in Figure 3.

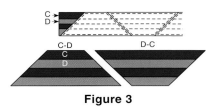

Figure 3

Step 9. Sew an E triangle to the short side of each C-D and D-C unit as shown in Figure 4; press seams toward E.

Figure 4

Step 10. Join a C-D-E unit with a D-C-E unit to complete a block center unit, again referring to Figure 4; press seam in one direction. Repeat to make four block center units.

Step 11. Sew F to G and add H to complete one side unit as shown in Figure 5; press seams toward F and H. Repeat to complete eight side units and eight reversed side units, again referring to Figure 5.

Figure 5

Completing the Topper

Step 1. Sew a side unit to opposite sides of a block center unit to complete a block center row as shown in Figure 6; press seams toward the center unit.

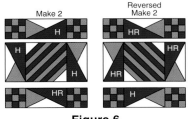

Figure 6

Easy Blue Table Topper
Placement Diagram
36" x 36"

Step 2. Sew an A corner unit to one end and a B corner unit to the remaining end of one side and one reversed side unit to make the block side rows, again referring to Figure 6; press seams toward the corner units.

Step 3. Sew the center row between the side rows to complete one Easy Blue block; press seams toward the center row. Repeat to make two blocks.

Step 4. Repeat Steps 1–3 using one side unit and three reversed side units to complete two Easy Blue Reversed blocks, again referring to Figure 6; press seams away from the center rows.

Step 5. Sew a block to a reversed block to make a row referring to the Placement Diagram for positioning of blocks; press seam toward the reversed block. Repeat for two rows.

Step 6. Join the rows to complete the top referring to the Placement Diagram for positioning; press seam to one side.

Step 7. Complete the quilt referring to Completing Your Quilt on page 170.

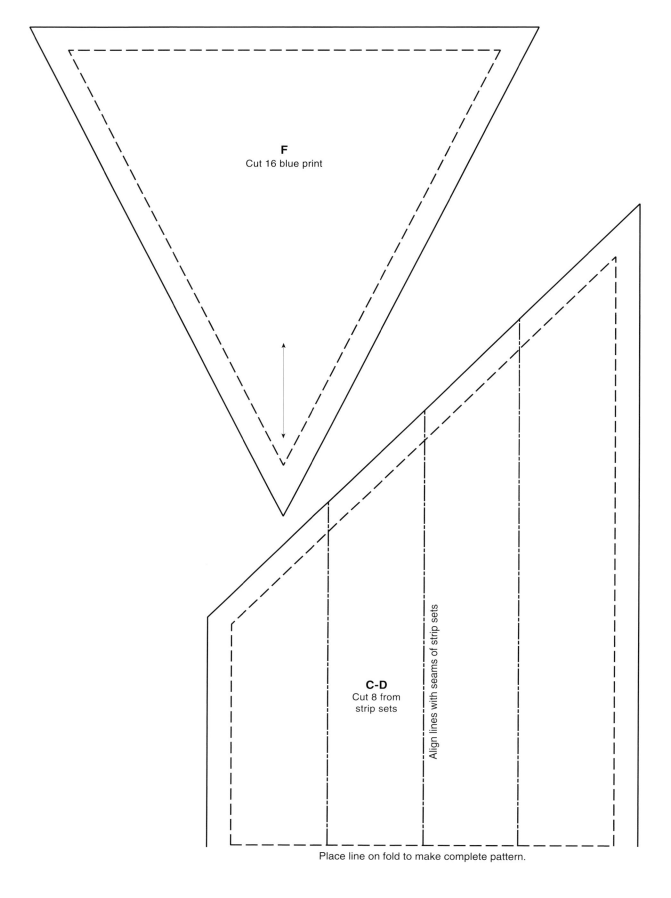

F
Cut 16 blue print

C-D
Cut 8 from
strip sets

Align lines with seams of strip sets

Place line on fold to make complete pattern.

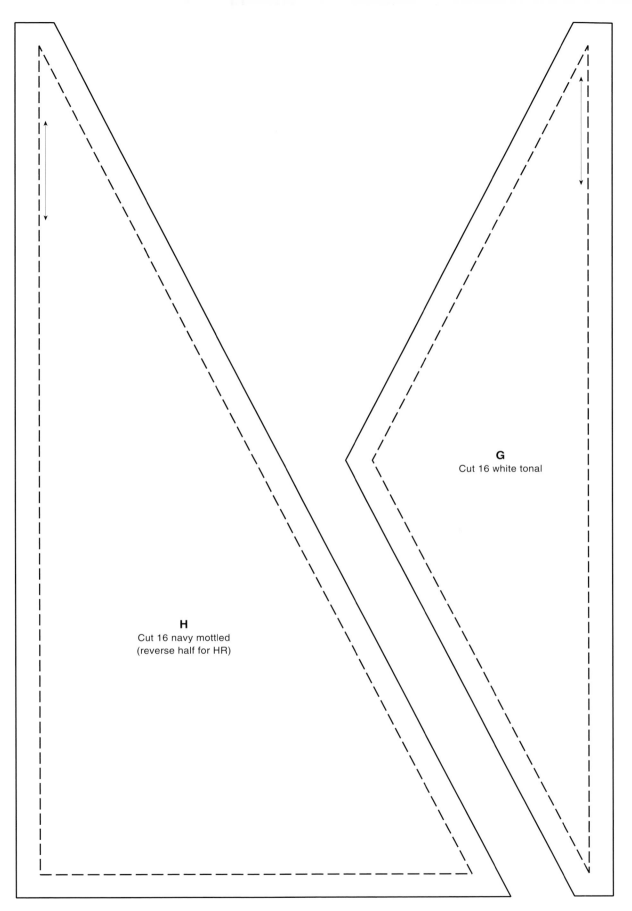

G
Cut 16 white tonal

H
Cut 16 navy mottled
(reverse half for HR)

Pansy Table Topper

Appliquéd pansies surround the scrappy-looking center of this table topper.

DESIGN BY BARBARA CLAYTON

Project Specifications
Skill Level: Intermediate
Topper Size: 44" x 44"

Materials
- 28 (4½" x 4½") A squares blue prints or tonals
- 28 (4½" x 4½") B squares green prints or tonals
- Scraps light, medium and dark blue prints or tonals for pansies
- Scrap gold for flower centers
- Scraps medium and dark green prints or tonals for leaves
- ⅝ yard cream tonal
- 1⅛ yards royal blue tonal
- Backing 50" x 50"
- Batting 50" x 50"
- All-purpose thread to match fabrics
- Quilting thread
- 1 yard 18"-wide fusible web
- Appliqué pressing sheet
- Basic sewing tools and supplies and water-erasable marker or pencil

Cutting
Step 1. Cut one 4½" by fabric width strip royal blue tonal; subcut strip into eight 4½" A squares.

Step 2. Cut two 1¾" x 32½" C strips and two 1¾" x 35" D strips royal blue tonal.

Step 3. Cut two 1¾" x 42" G strips and three 1¾" by fabric width strips royal blue tonal. Join the fabric-width strips to make one long strip; press seams open. Subcut strip into two 44½" H strips.

Step 4. Cut five 2¼" by fabric width strips royal blue tonal for binding.

Step 5. Cut two 4" x 35" E strips and two 4" x 42" F strips cream tonal.

Step 6. Prepare templates for appliqué shapes, adding seam allowance when pieces extend under other pieces as marked on the full-size motif.

Step 7. Trace shapes onto the paper side of the fusible web as directed on templates for number to cut; cut out shapes, leaving a margin around each piece.

Step 8. Fuse shapes to the wrong side of fabrics as directed on templates for color and number to cut; cut out shapes on traced lines. Remove paper backing.

Step 5. Sew G strips to opposite sides and H strips to the top and bottom of the pieced center; press seams toward the G and H strips.

Step 6. Trace a copy of the full-size pansy motif without leaves and place the copy under the appliqué pressing sheet. Prepare 16 pansy motifs on the appliqué pressing sheet using the full-size pattern as a guide for placement.

Step 7. Center a pansy motif with four leaves on each side on the E and F strips referring to the Placement Diagram for positioning; fuse shapes in place.

Step 8. Arrange three pansy motifs and four leaves at each corner referring to the Placement Diagram for positioning; fuse shapes in place.

Step 9. Referring to the Placement Diagram for positioning, transfer the quilting design given onto the E and F border strips using the water-erasable marker or pencil, centering the design between the pansy/leaf motifs.

Step 10. Complete the topper referring to Completing Your Quilt on page 170.

Step 11. Using thread to match fabrics, machine zigzag-stitch around the edges of each appliqué shape. ❖

Completing the Topper

Step 1. Arrange the A and B squares in rows by color referring to Figure 1; join in rows. Press seams in adjacent rows in opposite directions.

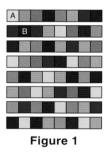

Figure 1

Step 2. Join the rows to complete the pieced center; press seams in one direction.

Step 3. Sew C strips to opposite sides and D strips to the top and bottom of the pieced center; press seams toward the C and D strips.

Step 4. Sew E strips to opposite sides and F strips to the top and bottom of the pieced center; press seams toward the E and F strips.

Pansy Table Topper
Placement Diagram
44" x 44"

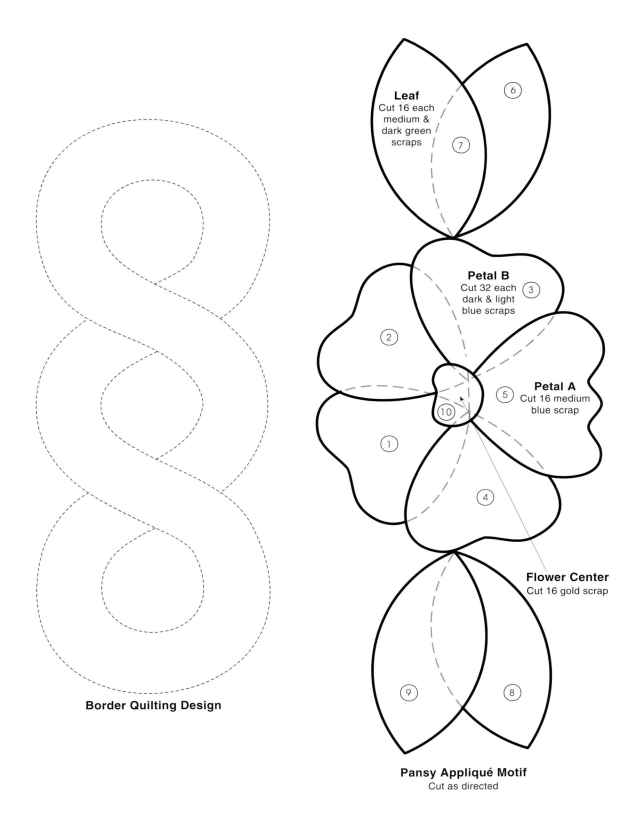

Leaf
Cut 16 each
medium &
dark green
scraps

Petal B
Cut 32 each
dark & light
blue scraps

Petal A
Cut 16 medium
blue scrap

Flower Center
Cut 16 gold scrap

Border Quilting Design

Pansy Appliqué Motif
Cut as directed

Sunny Day Topper

Brighten any day with this summery-looking table topper.

DESIGN BY CONNIE KAUFFMAN

Project Specifications
Skill Level: Beginner
Topper Size: 32" x 16"

Materials
- 1 fat quarter each yellow, blue, green and multicolor prints
- Backing 38" x 22"
- Batting 38" x 22"
- All-purpose thread to match fabrics
- Quilting thread
- Basic sewing tools and supplies

Cutting
Step 1. Cut (22) 2⅞" x 2⅞" A squares yellow print.
Step 2. Cut one 4⅛" x 4⅛" square each yellow (F) and blue (G) prints; cut each square on both diagonals to make four each F and G triangles.
Step 3. Cut (28) 2⅞" x 2⅞" B squares blue print.
Step 4. Cut (20) 2⅞" x 2⅞" C squares green print.
Step 5. Cut (10) 2⅞" x 2⅞" D squares multicolor print.
Step 6. Cut seven 5¼" x 5¼" squares multicolor print; cut each square on both diagonals to make 28 E triangles.

Completing the Topper
Step 1. Cut all A, B, C and D squares in half on one diagonal to make triangles.
Step 2. Join triangles on the diagonals as shown in Figure 1 to make triangle units; press seams toward darker fabric.

Figure 1

Step 3. Sew A, B, C and D triangles to E to make rectangle units as shown in Figure 2; press seams away from E.

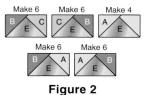

Figure 2

Step 4. Join the triangle units to make four-unit sections as shown in Figure 3; press seams in one direction.

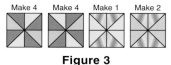

Figure 3

Step 5. Join the rectangle units to make square units as shown in Figure 4; press seams in one direction.

Make 6   Make 4

Figure 4

Step 6. Arrange the four-unit sections with the square units in rows with the remaining rectangle and triangle units and the F and G triangles referring to Figure 5; press seams in one direction.

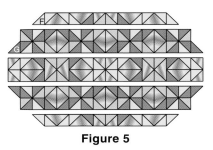

Figure 5

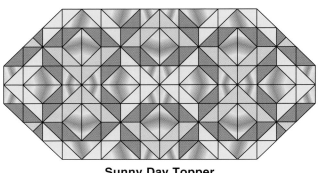

Sunny Day Topper
Placement Diagram
32" x 16"

Step 7. Trim off the B-C end units even with the angles of F and G as shown in Figure 6 to complete the top.

Figure 6

Step 8. Place the batting and backing right side up and topper right side down.

Step 9. Stitch all around outside edge of topper, leaving a 3" opening on one side. Trim batting and backing even with the topper edge.

Step 10. Turn topper right side out through the opening; press flat.

Step 11. Press opening edges inside ¼"; hand-stitch opening closed.

Step 12. Quilt as desired by hand or machine to finish. ❖

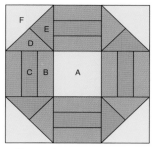

Wine London Roads
9" x 9" Block
Make 5

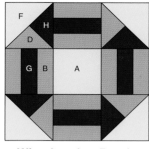

Green London Roads
9" x 9" Block
Make 4

London Roads

One block in two color variations make up this quick-to-stitch wall quilt or table topper. Select the outside border fabric first.

DESIGN BY JILL REBER

Project Specifications

Skill Level: Beginner
Quilt Size: 41" x 41"
Block Size: 9" x 9"
Number of Blocks: 9

Materials

- ⅜ yard green tonal
- ⅜ yard wine tonal
- ½ yard salmon tonal
- ¾ yard tan tonal
- 1⅛ yards salmon floral
- Backing 47" x 47"
- Batting 47" x 47"
- All-purpose thread to match fabrics
- Quilting thread
- Basic sewing tools and supplies

Cutting

Step 1. Cut one 3½" by fabric width strip tan tonal; subcut strip into nine 3½" A squares.

Step 2. Cut two 3⅞" by fabric width strips tan tonal; subcut strips into (18) 3⅞" squares. Cut each square in half on one diagonal to make 36 F triangles.

Step 3. Cut two 2½" x 27½" I strips and two 2½" x 31½" J strips tan tonal.

Step 4. Cut six 1½" by fabric width B strips salmon tonal; cut two strips in half to make four 1½" x 21" B strips.

Step 5. Cut one 4¼" by fabric width strip salmon tonal; subcut strip into nine 4¼" squares. Cut each square on both diagonals to make 36 D triangles.

Step 6. Cut one 4¼" by fabric width strip each green (E) and wine (H) tonals; subcut strips into four 4¼" E squares and five 4¼" H squares. Cut each square on both diagonals to make 16 E and 20 H triangles.

Step 7. Cut two 1½" by fabric width strips each green (C) and wine (G) tonals. Cut one C and G strip in half to make two 1½" x 21" each C and G strips; set aside one each half-C and half-G strips for another project.

Step 8. Cut two 5½" x 31½" K strips and two 5½" x 41½" L strips salmon floral.

Step 9. Cut five 2¼" by fabric width strips salmon floral for binding.

Completing the Blocks

Step 1. Sew a fabric-width C strip between two fabric-width B strips with right sides together along the length to make a B-C strip set; press seams toward the B strips.

Repeat with the half-C and two half-B strips to make a B-C half-strip set.

Step 2. Subcut the B-C strip sets into (16) 3½" B-C units as shown in Figure 1.

Figure 1

Step 3. Repeat Step 1 with B and G strips to make B-G strip sets.

Step 4. Subcut the B-G strip sets into (20) 3½" B-G units, again referring to Figure 1.

Step 5. To complete one Green London Roads block, sew D to E as shown in Figure 2; press seam toward E. Repeat to make four D-E units.

Figure 2   **Figure 3**

Step 6. Sew a D-E unit to F as shown in Figure 3; press seam toward F. Repeat to make four D-E-F units.

Step 7. Sew a D-E-F unit to opposite sides of a B-C unit to complete a row as shown in Figure 4; press seams away from the B-C unit. Repeat to make two rows.

Figure 4   **Figure 5**

Step 8. Sew a B-C unit to opposite sides of A as shown in Figure 5 to complete the center row; press seams toward A.

Step 9. Sew the center row between the two pieced rows referring to Figure 6 to complete one green block; press seams toward the center row. Repeat to make four Green London Roads blocks.

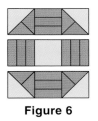

Figure 6

Step 10. Repeat Steps 5–8 with D, H and F triangles, B-G units and A referring to Figure 7 to make five Wine London Roads blocks. Press seams away from the center row.

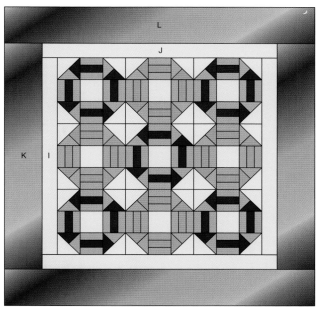

London Roads
Placement Diagram
41" x 41"

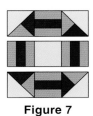

Figure 7

Completing the Quilt

Step 1. Join two wine blocks with one green block to make a wine row referring to the Placement Diagram for positioning; press seams toward the wine blocks. Repeat to make two wine rows.

Step 2. Repeat Step 1 with two green blocks and one wine block to make one row; press seams toward the wine block.

Step 3. Join the rows referring to the Placement Diagram for positioning; press seams in one direction.

Step 4. Sew an I strip to opposite sides and J strips to the remaining sides of the pieced center; press seams toward the I and J strips.

Step 5. Sew a K strip to opposite sides and L strips to the remaining sides of the pieced center to complete the pieced top; press seams toward K and L strips.

Step 6. Complete the quilt referring to Completing Your Quilt on page 170. ❖

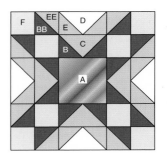

Mom's Kitchen
12" x 12" Block

Mom's Kitchen

The use of reproduction fabrics brings back memories of my mother's kitchen. This star design looks just as good in today's fabrics.

DESIGN BY JULIE WEAVER

Project Specifications
Skill Level: Beginner
Quilt Size: 60" x 60"
Block Size: 12" x 12"
Number of Blocks: 12

Materials
- ½ yard green print
- ¾ yard green floral
- 1 yard green/white dot
- 1⅛ yards red check tonal
- 1¼ yards light green tonal
- 1½ yards cream tonal
- Backing 66" x 66"
- Batting 66" x 66"
- All-purpose thread to match fabrics
- Quilting thread
- Basic sewing tools and supplies

Cutting
Step 1. Cut two 4½" by fabric width strips green floral; subcut strips into (12) 4½" A squares.
Step 2. Cut one 12½" x 12½" G square green floral.
Step 3. Cut six 2½" by fabric width strips each red check (B) and light green (E) tonals; subcut strips into (96) 2½" squares each fabric for B and E. Draw a diagonal line from corner to corner on the wrong side of all squares.
Step 4. Cut four 2⅞" by fabric width strips each red check (BB) and light green (EE) tonals; subcut strips into (48) 2⅞" squares each fabric. Draw a diagonal line from corner to corner on the wrong side of each EE square.
Step 5. Cut nine 1" by fabric width strips red check tonal. Join strips on short ends to make one long strip; press seams open. Subcut strip into two strips each in the following sizes: 12½" H, 13½" I, 23½" P, 24½" Q, 48½" R and 49½" S.
Step 6. Cut three 4½" by fabric width strips each light green (C) and cream (D) tonals; subcut strips into 48 each 2½" C and D rectangles.
Step 7. Cut six 2½" by fabric width strips green print; subcut strips into (96) 2½" F squares.
Step 8. Cut eight 4½" by fabric width strips cream tonal; subcut each of two of these strips into one 14½" L strip and one 22½" M strip to total two L and two M strips. Join the remaining six strips on the short ends to make one long strip; press seams open. Subcut strips into two 50½" V strips and two 58½" W strips.
Step 9. Cut nine 1" by fabric width strips green/white

dot. Join strips on short ends to make one long strip; press seams open. Subcut strip into two strips each in the following sizes: 13½" J, 14½" K, 22½" N, 23½" O, 49½" T and 50½" U.

Step 10. Cut six 1½" by fabric width strips green/white dot. Join strips on short ends to make one long strip; press seams open. Subcut strip into two 58½" X strips and two 60½" Y strips.

Step 11. Cut six 2¼" by fabric width strips green/white dot for binding.

Completing the Blocks

Step 1. Referring to Figure 1, place a B square right sides together on one end of C; stitch on the marked line. Trim seam to ¼" and press B to the right side. Repeat on the opposite end of C to complete one B-C unit. Repeat to make 48 units.

Step 2. Repeat Step 1 with D and E pieces to complete 48 D-E units, again referring to Figure 1.

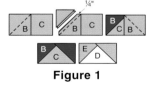

Figure 1

Step 3. Referring to Figure 2, place an EE square right sides together with a BB square; stitch ¼" on each side of the marked line. Cut apart on the marked line to make two BB-EE units. Repeat with all BB and EE squares to make 96 units.

Figure 2

Step 4. To complete one Mom's Kitchen block, join one D-E unit with one B-C unit to make a side unit as shown in Figure 3; press seam toward the B-C unit. Repeat to make four side units.

Figure 3

Step 5. Sew a BB-EE unit to F as shown in Figure 4; press seam toward F. Repeat. Join the two units to complete a corner unit, again referring to Figure 4. Press seam in one direction. Repeat to make four corner units.

Figure 4

Step 6. Sew a side unit between two corner units to make the top row as shown in Figure 5; press seams toward corner units. Repeat to make the bottom row.

Make 2

Make 1

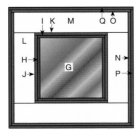

Figure 5

Step 7. Sew a side row to opposite sides of A to complete the center row as shown in Figure 5; press seams toward A.

Step 8. Sew the center row between the top and bottom rows to complete one block; repeat to make 12 blocks. Press seams toward the center row in six blocks and away from the center row in six blocks.

Completing the Quilt
Step 1. Sew H–Q strips to G in alphabetical order to complete the G unit referring to Figure 6; press seams toward strips after each addition.

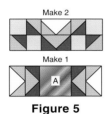

Figure 6

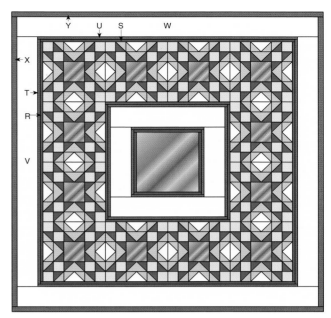

Mom's Kitchen
Placement Diagram
60" x 60"

Step 2. Join four blocks to make a row; press seams in one direction. Repeat to make two rows.

Step 3. Join two blocks to make a side row; press seam in one direction. Repeat to make two side rows.

Step 4. Sew a side row to opposite sides of the G unit to complete the center row; press seams toward the G unit.

Step 5. Join the rows to complete the pieced center; press seams toward the center row.

Step 6. Sew the R–Y strips to the pieced center in alphabetical order to complete the quilt top; press seams toward strips after each addition.

Step 7. Complete the quilt referring to Completing Your Quilt on page 170. ❖

Flower Table Topper

This topper takes the shape of a flower. Let it bloom on your table!

DESIGN BY CONNIE RAND

Project Specifications
Skill Level: Intermediate
Topper Size: 36" x 36"

Materials
- 1 (2" x 20") strip each 2 different green prints or tonals (H)
- ⅓ yard white tonal
- ⅓ yard each green check and green mottled batiks
- 1 yard navy mottled
- Backing 40" x 40"
- Batting 40" x 40"
- All-purpose thread to match fabrics
- Quilting thread
- Template material
- Basic sewing tools and supplies

Cutting
Step 1. Cut one 13¼" by fabric width strip navy mottled; subcut strip into one 13¼" A square and four 5⅜" F squares. Cut each F square in half on one diagonal to make eight F triangles.

Step 2. Cut four 2" by fabric width strips navy mottled; set aside one strip for I. Subcut the remaining strips into nine 9½" G strips.

Step 3. Cut four 2¼" by fabric width strips navy mottled for binding.

Step 4. Cut one 2" x 20" H strip each green mottled and green check batiks.

Step 5. Cut one 5⅜" by fabric width strip green check batik; subcut strip into two 5⅜" squares. Cut each square in half on one diagonal to make four D triangles.

Step 6. Cut one 7¼" by fabric width strip green mottled batik; subcut strip into four 7¼" squares. Cut each square in half on one diagonal to make eight E triangles.

Step 7. Cut one 4¼" by fabric width J strip white tonal.

Step 8. Prepare templates for B and C pieces; cut as directed on patterns.

Piecing the Units
Step 1. Sew B to C to D as shown in Figure 1; press seams away from B. Repeat to make four B-C-D units.

Make 4

Figure 1

Step 2. Sew a B-C-D unit to each side of A to complete the center unit referring to Figure 2; press seams toward A.

Figure 2

Step 3. Join the four H strips with right sides together along length to make a strip set; press seams in one direction.

Step 4. Cut the strip set into four 4¼" H units as shown in Figure 3.

Figure 3

Step 5. Sew F to one short side of E and add G to the long side of E to complete an E-F-G unit as shown in Figure 4; press seams toward F and G. Repeat to make four units and four reversed units, again referring to Figure 4.

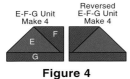

Figure 4

Step 6. Join the I and J strips with right sides together along length to make a strip set; press seam toward I.

Step 7. Cut the strip set into four 6½" I-J units as shown in Figure 5.

Figure 5

Completing the Topper

Step 1. Sew an H unit to the I side of an I-J unit to complete an H-I-J unit as shown in Figure 6; press seam toward I. Repeat to make four units.

Figure 6

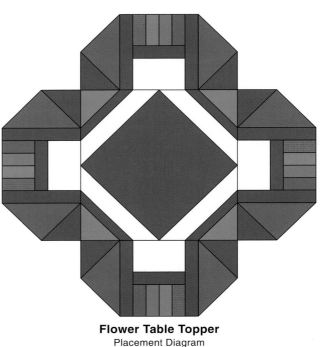

Flower Table Topper
Placement Diagram
36" x 36"

Step 2. Sew an E-F-G unit to one side and a reversed E-F-G unit to the opposite side of each H-I-J unit to complete four side units as shown in Figure 7; press seams toward G.

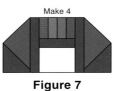

Figure 7

Step 3. Sew a side unit to each side of the center unit to complete the top; press seams toward the center unit.

Step 4. Layer, quilt and prepare binding strips referring to Completing Your Quilt on page 170.
Note: *To bind inside corners, stitch to the corner where seam allowances would intersect and stop, leaving the needle down. Raise the presser foot, pivot the top and align the binding with the edge of the top again and continue stitching. When turning to the back side, pleat excess as if mitering seams on a corner.* ❖

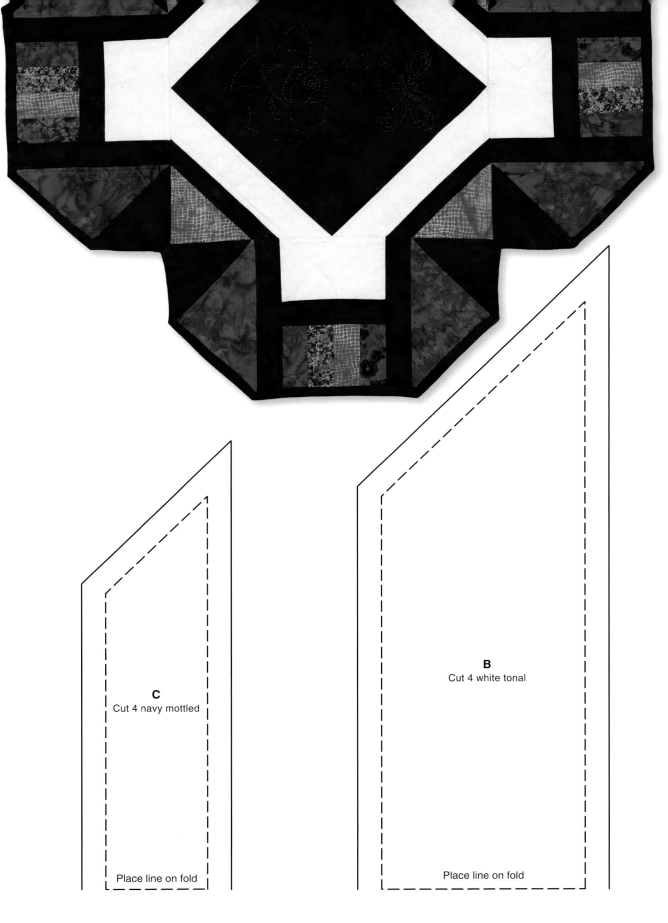

C
Cut 4 navy mottled

Place line on fold

B
Cut 4 white tonal

Place line on fold

General Instructions

Finishing the Top
Adding Borders

Borders are an integral part of the quilt and should complement the colors and designs used in the quilt center. Borders frame a quilt just like a mat and frame do a picture. Individual projects include cutting instructions for borders, but you may want to change them to suit your own size requirements. The instructions that follow will help you cut accurate-size strips.

Border strips may be mitered or butted at the corners as shown in Figures 1 and 2. To determine the size for butted border strips, measure across the center of the completed quilt top from the top raw edge to the bottom raw edge. This measurement will include a ¼" seam allowance.

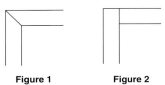

Figure 1   **Figure 2**

Cut two border strips that length by the chosen width of the border. Sew these strips to the opposite sides of the pieced center referring to Figure 3. Press the seam allowance toward border strips.

Figure 3

Measure across the completed quilt top at the center, from one side raw edge to the other side raw edge, including the two border strips added. Cut two border strips that length by the chosen width of the border. Sew a strip to the top and bottom, again referring to Figure 3. Press the seams toward border strips.

To make mitered corners, measure the quilt as before.

To this add twice the width of the border and ½" for seam allowances to determine the length of the strips. Repeat for opposite sides. Center and sew on each strip, stopping stitching ¼" from each corner and leaving the remainder of the strip dangling as shown in Figure 4.

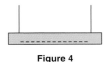

Figure 4

Referring to Figures 5–7, press corners at a 45-degree angle to form a crease. Align border strips right sides together; stitch from the inside quilt corner to the outside on the creased line. Trim excess away after stitching and press mitered seams open.

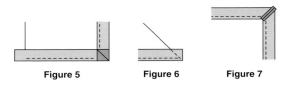

Figure 5   **Figure 6**   **Figure 7**

Carefully press the entire piece, including the pieced center. Avoid pulling and stretching while pressing, which would distort shapes.

Completing Your Quilt
Choosing a Quilting Design

If you choose to hand- or machine-quilt your finished top, you will need to choose a design for quilting.

There are several types of quilting designs, some of which may not have to be marked. The easiest of the unmarked designs is in-the-ditch quilting. Here the quilting stitches are placed in the valley created by the seams joining two pieces together or next to the edge of an appliqué design. There is no need to mark a top for in-the-ditch quilting. Machine quilters choose this option because the stitches are not as obvious on the finished quilt (Figure 8).

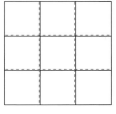

Figure 8

Outline-quilting ¼" or more away from seams or appliqué shapes is another no-mark alternative (Figure 9) that prevents having to sew through the layers made by seams, thus making stitching easier.

Figure 9

If you are not comfortable eyeballing the ¼" (or other distance), masking tape is available in different widths and is helpful to place on straight-edge designs to mark the quilting line. If using masking tape, place the tape right up against the seam and quilt close to the other edge.

Meander or free-motion quilting by machine (Figure 10) fills in open spaces and doesn't require marking. It is fun and easy to stitch.

Figure 10

Marking the Top for Quilting

If you choose a fancy or allover design for quilting, you will need to transfer the design to your quilt top before layering with the backing and batting.

You may use a sharp medium-lead or silver pencil on light background fabrics. Test the pencil marks to guarantee that they will wash out of your quilt top when quilting is complete, or be sure your quilting stitches cover the pencil marks. Mechanical pencils with very fine points may be used successfully to mark quilts.

Many quilters have discovered that a silver pencil works well for marking quilting designs on quilt tops. Many quilt shops carry these pencils so you won't have to buy a set of colored pencils just to get one color!

Manufactured quilting-design templates are available in many designs and sizes and are cut out of a durable plastic template material that is easy to use.

To make a permanent quilting-design template, choose a template material on which to transfer the design. See-through plastic is the best because it will let you place the design while allowing you to see where it is in relation to your quilt design without moving it. Trace the design on the template material and either cut out the shape or just cut slits in the template material on the traced lines through which a pencil may be inserted. Place the prepared template on the quilt top where you want it and trace around it with your marking tool. Pick up the quilting template and place again; repeat marking.

No matter what marking method you use, remember—the marked lines should never show on the finished quilt. When the top is marked, it is ready for layering.

Preparing the Quilt Backing

The quilt backing is a very important feature of your quilt. In most cases, the Materials list for each quilt in this book gives the size requirements for the backing, not the yardage needed. Exceptions to this are when the backing fabric is also used on the quilt top and yardage is given for both the top and backing in one amount.

A backing is generally cut at least 6" larger than the quilt top or 3" larger on all sides. For a 64" x 78" finished quilt, the backing would need to be at least 70" x 84".

To avoid having the seam down the center of the back, cut two fabric pieces the length of the backing needed; cut or tear one of these pieces in half, and sew half to each side of the second piece as shown in Figure 11.

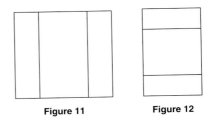

Figure 11   **Figure 12**

Quilt backings that are more than 88" wide may be pieced in horizontal pieces as shown in Figure 12.

Layering the Quilt Sandwich

Layering the quilt top with the batting and backing is time-consuming. Open the batting several days before you need it and place over a bed or flat on the floor to help flatten the creases caused from folds from packaging.

Iron the backing piece, folding in half both vertically and horizontally and pressing to mark the centers.

If you will not be quilting on a frame, place the backing right side down on a clean floor or table. Start in the center and push any wrinkles or bunches flat. Use masking tape to tape the edges to the floor or large clips to hold the backing to the edge of the tables. The backing should be taut.

Place the batting on top of the backing, matching centers using fold lines as guides; flatten out any wrinkles. Trim the batting to the same size as the backing. Fold the quilt top in half lengthwise and place on top of the batting, wrong side against the batting, matching centers. Unfold quilt and, working from the center to the outside edges, smooth out any wrinkles or lumps.

To hold the quilt layers together for quilting, baste by hand or use safety pins. If basting by hand, thread a long thin needle with a long piece of unknotted white or off-white thread. Starting in the center and leaving a long tail, make 4"–6"-long stitches toward the outside edge of the quilt top, smoothing as you baste. Start at the center again and work toward the outside as shown in Figure 13.

Figure 13

If quilting by machine, you may prefer to use safety pins to hold your fabric sandwich together. To use pins, start in the center of the quilt and pin to the outside, leaving pins open until all are placed. When you are satisfied that all layers are smooth, close the pins. To use basting spray, follow the manufacturer's instructions on the container.

Quilting
Hand Quilting

Hand quilting is the process of placing stitches through the quilt top, batting and backing to hold them together. While it serves a functional purpose, it also adds beauty and loft to the finished quilt.

To begin, thread a sharp between needle with an 18" piece of quilting thread. Tie a small knot in the end of the thread. Position the needle about ½"–1" away from the starting point on the quilt top. Sink needle through the top into the batting layer but not through the backing. Pull the needle up at the starting point of the quilting design. Pull the needle and thread until the knot sinks through the top into the batting (Figure 14).

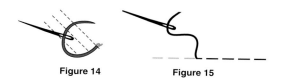

Figure 14   **Figure 15**

Some stitchers like to take a backstitch right at the beginning while others prefer to begin the first stitch here. Take small, even running stitches along the marked quilting line (Figure 15). Keep one hand positioned underneath to feel the needle go all the way through to the backing.

When you have nearly run out of thread, wind the thread around the needle several times to make a small knot and pull it close to the fabric. Insert the needle into the fabric on the quilting line and come out with the needle ½"–1" away, pulling the knot into the fabric layers the same as when you started. Pull and cut thread close to fabric. The end should disappear inside after cutting. Some quilters prefer to take a backstitch with a loop through it for a knot to end.

Machine Quilting

Successful machine quilting requires practice and a good relationship with your sewing machine. Special machine-quilting needles work best to penetrate the three layers in your quilt.

Prepare the quilt for machine quilting in the same way as for hand quilting. Use safety pins to hold the layers together instead of basting with thread.

Presser-foot quilting is best used for straight-line quilting because the presser bar lever does not need to be continually lifted. Set the machine on a longer stitch length (3.0 or 8–10 stitches to the inch). Too tight a stitch causes puckering and fabric tucks, either on the quilt top or backing. An even-feed or walking foot helps to eliminate the tucks and puckering by feeding the upper and lower layers through the machine evenly. Before you begin, loosen the amount of pressure on the presser foot.

For free-motion quilting, use your machine's darning foot with the feed dogs down. Refer to your sewing machine manual for other special instructions. Practice on a sample before trying this method on your quilt.

Finishing the Edges

After your quilt is quilted, the edges need to be finished, but you must decide how you want the edges of your quilt finished before layering the backing and batting with the quilt top.

Without Binding—Self-Finish

There are several ways to eliminate adding an edge finish. This is done before quilting. Place the batting on a flat surface. Place the pieced top right side up on the batting. Place the backing right sides together with the pieced top. Pin and/or baste the layers together to hold flat referring to Layering the Quilt Sandwich.

Begin stitching in the center of one side using a ¼" seam allowance, reversing at the beginning and end of the seam. Continue stitching all around and back to the beginning side. Leave a 12" or larger opening. Clip corners to reduce excess. Turn right side out through the opening. Turn the raw edges in ¼" and slipstitch the opening closed by hand. The quilt may now be quilted by hand or machine.

The disadvantage to this method is that once the edges are stitched, any creases or wrinkles that might form during the quilting process cannot be flattened out. Tying is the preferred method for finishing a quilt constructed using this method.

There are several self-finishing methods that use the edges of the quilt top or backing. Bringing the backing fabric to the front is one of these methods. To accomplish this, complete the quilt as for hand or machine quilting. Trim only the batting even with the quilt top. Trim the backing 1" larger than the completed top all around.

Turn the backing edge ½" to the wrong side; fold to overlap onto the front of the quilt ¼". The folded edge may be machine-stitched close to the edge through all layers, or blind-stitched in place to finish.

The front may be turned to the back. If using this method, a wider front border is needed. The backing and batting are trimmed 1" smaller than the top, and the top edge is turned under ½" and then turned to the back and stitched in place.

One more method of self-finish may be used. The top and backing may be stitched together by hand at the edge. To accomplish this, quilting must be stopped ½" from the quilt-top edge. The top and backing of the quilt are trimmed even and the batting is trimmed to ¼"–½" smaller. The edges of the top and backing are turned in ¼"–½" and blind-stitched together at the very edge.

These methods do not require the use of extra fabric and save time in preparation of binding strips; they are not as durable as an added binding.

Binding

The technique of adding extra fabric at the edges of the quilt is called binding. The binding encloses the edges and adds an extra layer of fabric for durability. The instructions given with most of the projects in this book list cutting for a number of 2¼"-wide binding strips. Use these strips and follow the instructions for double-fold, straight-grain binding to finish, or create binding using one of the other following methods.

To prepare a quilt for the addition of the binding, trim the batting and backing layers even with the top of the quilt using a rotary cutter and ruler or shears. Using a walking-foot attachment (sometimes called an even-feed foot attachment), machine-baste the three layers together all around approximately ⅛" from the cut edge.

Bias binding may be purchased in packages in many different colors but is not always available in a color to match your quilt. The advantage to self-made binding is that you can use fabrics from your quilt to coordinate colors.

Double-fold, straight-grain binding and double-fold, bias-grain binding are two of the most commonly used types of binding.

Double-fold, straight-grain binding is commonly used on the edges of quilts with square corners. Double-fold, bias-grain binding is best suited for quilts with rounded corners or scalloped edges.

Making & Applying Straight-Grain Binding

To make double-fold, straight-grain binding, cut 2¼"-wide strips of fabric across the width or down the length of the fabric totaling the perimeter of the quilt plus 12". The strips are joined as shown in Figure 16 and pressed in half wrong sides together along the length using an iron on a cotton setting with no steam.

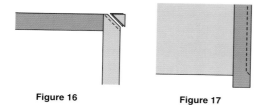

Figure 16   Figure 17

Lining up the raw edges, place the binding on the top of the quilt and begin sewing (again using the walking foot) approximately 6" from the beginning of the binding strip. Stop sewing ¼" from the first corner, leave the needle in the quilt, turn and sew diagonally to the corner as shown in Figure 17.

Fold the binding at a 45-degree angle up and away from the quilt as shown in Figure 18 and back down even with the raw edge of the next side of the quilt. Starting at the top raw edge of the quilt, begin sewing the next side as shown in Figure 19. Repeat at the next three corners.

Figure 18   Figure 19

As you approach the beginning of the binding strip, stop stitching and overlap the binding ends ½"; trim. Join the two ends with a ¼" seam allowance and press the seam open. Reposition the joined binding along the edge of the quilt and resume stitching to the beginning.

To finish, bring the folded edge of the binding over the raw edges and blind-stitch the binding in place over the machine-stitching line on the back side. Hand-miter the corners on the back as shown in Figure 20.

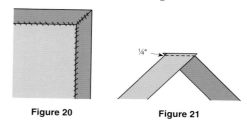

Figure 20   Figure 21

Making & Applying Bias-Grain Binding

To make double-fold, bias-grain binding, cut 2¼"-wide bias strips from the binding-fabric yardage. Join the strips as shown in Figure 21 and press seams open. Fold the joined strips in half with wrong sides together along the length, and press with no steam as for straight-grain binding.

Follow the same procedures as previously described for preparing the quilt top and sewing the binding to the quilt top. Treat the corners just as instructed for straight-grain binding.

Since you are using bias-grain binding, you do have the option to just eliminate the corners if it doesn't interfere with the patchwork in the quilt. Round the corners off by placing a dinner plate at the corner and rotary-cutting the gentle curve (Figure 22).

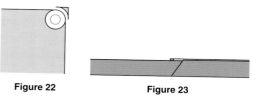

Figure 22   Figure 23

As you approach the beginning of the binding strip, stop stitching and lay the end across the beginning so it will slip inside the fold. Cut the end at a 45-degree angle so the raw edges are contained inside the beginning of the strip (Figure 23). Resume stitching to the beginning. Bring the fold to the back of the quilt and hand-stitch as previously described.

Overlapped corners are also easier than mitered corners. To make overlapped corners, sew binding strips to opposite sides of the quilt top. Turn the folded edge to the back side and stitch edges down to finish. Trim ends even.

Sew a strip to each remaining side, leaving 1½"–2" excess at each end. Turn quilt over and fold binding end in even with previous finished edge as shown in Figure 24.

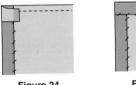

| Figure 24 | Figure 25 |

Fold binding over onto quilt back and stitch down as before, enclosing the previous bound edge in the seam as shown in Figure 25. It may be necessary to trim the folded-down section to reduce bulk.

Making Continuous Bias Binding

Instead of cutting individual bias strips and sewing them together, you may make continuous bias binding.

Cut a square 18" x 18" from chosen binding fabric. Cut the square in half on one diagonal to make two triangles as shown in Figure 26. With right sides together, join the two triangles with a ¼" seam allowance as shown in Figure 27; press seam open to reduce bulk.

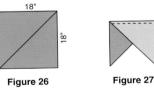

| Figure 26 | Figure 27 |

Mark lines every 2¼" on the wrong side of the fabric as shown in Figure 28. Bring the short ends right sides together, offsetting one line as shown in Figure 29; stitch to make a tube. This will seem awkward.

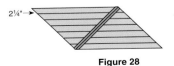

Figure 28

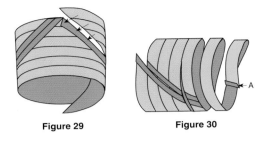

| Figure 29 | Figure 30 |

Begin cutting at point A as shown in Figure 30; continue cutting along marked line to make one continuous strip. Fold strip in half along length with wrong sides together; press. Sew to quilt edges as instructed previously for bias binding.

Final Touches

If your quilt will be hung on the wall, a hanging sleeve, purchased plastic rings or fabric tabs are needed. The best choice is a fabric sleeve that will evenly distribute the weight of the quilt across the top edge, rather than at selected spots where tabs or rings are stitched, keep the quilt hanging straight and not damage the batting.

To make a sleeve, measure across the top of the finished quilt. Cut an 8"-wide piece of muslin equal to that length—you may need to join several muslin strips to make the required length.

Fold in ¼" on each end of the muslin strip and press. Fold again and stitch to hold. Fold the muslin strip with right sides together along the length. Sew along the long side to make a tube. Turn the tube right side out; press with seam at bottom or centered on the back.

Hand-stitch the top of the tube along the top of the quilt and the bottom of the tube to the quilt back, making sure the quilt lies flat. Stitches should not go through to the front of the quilt and don't need to be too close together. Slip a wooden dowel or long curtain rod through the sleeve to hang.

When the quilt is finally complete, it should be signed and dated. Use a permanent pen on the back of the quilt. Other methods include cross-stitching your name and date on the front or back or making a permanent label that may be stitched to the back. ❖

Special Thanks

We would like to thank the talented quilt designers whose work is featured in this collection.

Fabrics & Supplies

Page 13: Little Miss Toy Tote—Sulky metallic and rayon threads and Steam-A-Seam2 double stick fusible web.

Page 17: Lullaby—Hobbs Thermore batting.

Page 19: Dragonfly Baby Quilt—Pellon Wonder-Under fusible web and Stitch-N-Tear fabric stabilizer, Quilter's Grid gridded fusible web and Fiskar's rotary-cutting tools.

Page 22: Rainbow Baby Quilt—60/40 Machine Blend batting from Fairfield Processing and Star Machine Quilting thread from Coats.

Page 25: Neon Fabric Fun—Master Piece 45 ruler and Static Stickers.

Page 28: Doggie Dreams—Changing Seasons fabric collection from Classic Cottons, Warm & Natural cotton batting from The Warm Co., Dual Duty Plus all-purpose and Star Machine Quilting thread from Coats and Quilt Basting Spray from Sullivans USA.

Page 33: Scotties on Parade—Changing Seasons fabric collection from Classic Cottons, Warm & Natural cotton batting from The Warm Co., Dual Duty Plus all-purpose and Star Machine Quilting thread from Coats and Quilt Basting Spray from Sullivans USA.

Page 41: Fat Quarter Floral Throw—Hobbs Heirloom Fusible batting and Sulky cotton and variegated threads.

Page 45: Split Log Cabin—Jazz Club stripe and dotted fabrics from Quilting Treasures, 60/40 Machine Blend batting from Fairfield Processing and Star Machine Quilting thread from Coats.

Page 51: Crossroads—Iditarod fabric collection by Adrienne Yorinks for Lyndhurst Studio and Presencia thread.

Page 62: Flower Power—Hobbs Thermore batting.

Page 76: Quilter's Delight—60/40 Machine Blend batting

from Fairfield Processing and Star Machine Quilting thread from Coats. Machine-quilted by Dianne Hodgkins.

Page 85: Christmas Ribbons—Cranston Village Heirloom Gallery fabric collection, 60/40 Machine Blend batting from Fairfield Processing and Star Machine Quilting thread from Coats.

Page 87: Mardi Gras Christmas—Marbled fabrics from Classic Cottons, Warm & Natural cotton batting from The Warm Co., Dual Duty Plus all-purpose Quilting and Craft thread from Coats and Quilt Basting Spray from Sullivans USA.

Page 90: Holiday Triangles—A Special Occasion fabric collection from RJR Fabrics, 60/40 Machine Blend batting from Fairfield Processing and Star Machine Quilting thread from Coats.

Page 95: Circle the Tree—Holiday Palette fabrics from Classic Cottons, Warm & Natural

cotton batting from The Warm Co., Dual Duty Plus all-purpose and Star Multicolored Quilting and Craft thread from Coats and Quilt Basting Spray from Sullivans USA.

Page 124: Tree Time Table Setting—Master Piece 45 ruler and Static Stickers and Presencia threads.

Page 139: Pleasingly Paisley Table Topper—Mansfield Park fabric collection from Timeless Treasures.

Page 147: Easy Blue Table Topper—Star Machine Quilting & Craft thread from Coats and 60/40 Machine Blend batting from Fairfield Processing.

Page 156: Sunny Day Topper—Hobbs Premium cotton batting and Sulky Sliver metallic thread.

Page 159: London Roads—Master Piece 45 ruler and Static Stickers and Presencia threads.

Page 162: Mom's Kitchen—Hobbs Thermore batting.